The Baby Boomers' Guide to Grandparenting

An Irreverent Look at the Next Big Step

DIANA J. EWING

The Baby Boomers' Guide to Grandparenting

An Irreverent Look at the Next Big Step

ISBN-10: 1453677577

Printed in the United States of America

The author is grateful for permission to reprint all song lyrics, as listed at the end of the book.

In loving memory of Marie and Vincent White,
the most wonderful grandparents
a baby boomer ever had.

And for Mom, who good-naturedly embraced
assorted dogs, cats, and parrots
as the next best thing to grandchildren.

Contents

Foreword

Let's get one thing straight right up front. I am NOT a grandma. I'm not even a mom. I say this now so you won't mistakenly assume I know what I'm talking about in the pages that follow.

Married late and with a biological clock that neglected to tick, I felt fine that I didn't have children. When my friends started having grandchildren, however, I wanted some of those little rascals for myself. Nana envy, I think they call it. By then, of course, it was too late to do anything about it, so I decided to write this book instead.

I had a pretty good handle on the baby-boomer part since I've been a boomer all my life, and grandparents across the country generously provided a wealth of stories and ideas to get this non-grandma started.

So if you're looking for grandparenting advice from someone who's actually been there, drop this book like a dirty diaper. But if you're ready for a rollicking ride through Grandparentland, with frequent detours down the boomer side of Memory Lane, then this is the book for you.

Happy Grandparenting!
Diana J. Ewing

Chapter 1
But We're Too Young To Be Grandparents

♫ Time keeps on slippin', slippin', slippin' into the future.♫

~Steve Miller

nce upon a time in the sixties we baby boomers vowed never to trust anybody over thirty. Now our own thirtysomething years are a distant memory, and we keep getting mail from AARP. Wait a minute, isn't that one of those organizations for *old* people? Clearly, somebody has made a mistake. We're still hip. We're still relevant. Our credentials are nothing but cool.

Weren't boomer gals glued to black-and-white TV sets across America every time The Beatles appeared on *The Ed Sullivan Show?* And right away didn't boomer guys start growing their hair longer accordingly?

Wasn't it us boomers who danced the full seventeen minutes to "In-A-Gadda-Da-Vida," having no idea what it meant? And weren't we the ones who drove our VW microbuses all the way to Woodstock? Okay, maybe some of us only saw the movie, but we were there in spirit. It doesn't get any cooler than that.

We were cutting-edge long before the phrase was invented, with our leather vests, tie-dyed T-shirts, Nehru jackets, and fringed bell-bottom jeans. Our love beads were both fashion statement and philosophy, and we took to wearing headbands as naturally as we had worn class rings and circle pins.

Our heroes were Batman and Captain Kirk, but we wanted to be Julie, Linc, and Pete on *The Mod Squad*. We knew Sean Connery was the ONLY James Bond, whether shaken or stirred, and we turned *Easy Rider* into a religious experience.

As we struggled to distinguish ourselves from the generations that came before, we were thrilled to learn that *I'm OK-You're OK*. Then we messed up our relationships anyway.

These were groundbreaking experiences back in the day. Way, way back. Sure, the sixties were happening, but they were happening a long time ago. Yes, *Hair* was the musical that defined our generation, but today it just keeps falling out. And hip is great until your doctor starts talking about a replacement.

Still, from the Age of Aquarius to the day of our first senior movie discount, we baby boomers have shown an amazing talent for reinventing ourselves and making every life stage uniquely our own. Since it's worked so well in the past, why should we approach grandparenting any differently?

THEN	NOW
Apples and oranges	Macs and PCs
Princess Grace	Queen Latifah
Bald guys out	Bald guys in
The Lennon Sisters	The Jonas Brothers
Walter Cronkite	Katie Couric
Rush to the bank by 3 p.m.	Drop by the ATM anytime
Mind your manners	Manners schmanners
Sing Along with Mitch	Dancing with the Stars
Too many telephone poles	Not enough cell towers
"You're welcome."	"No problem."

Now that the initial shock has worn off, let's take a look at how we ever managed to get here from there.

One minute we were soaring as free as *Jonathan Livingston Seagull*, making macramé plant hangers and baking special brownies in funky apartments decorated with batik fabrics and bookcases made of bricks and boards. Somebody was always strumming a guitar. "This Land Is Your Land." "Michael, Row the Boat Ashore." "Kumbaya." We knew all the words.

The next minute we had become decidedly earthbound, juggling jobs, families, and mortgages. Even as we acquired furniture groupings and began filling up our cabinets with Tupperware, we promised ourselves we'd never turn into our parents. Not as long as we kept the incense burning and The Doors and Jimi Hendrix records playing. It was our groovy version of real life.

Through teething and chicken pox, school carpools and proms, we somehow survived that giant, careening roller coaster known as parenthood. Now it's time for our kids to climb aboard this DNA-fueled ride of their lives. Intellectually we know our children

> ### *GRANECDOTE*
> #### *Grandparenting 101*
>
> *"When our son first learned that they were expecting, he very seriously asked his father and me if we planned to take grandparenting classes. Our reply: 'Are you crazy?'"*
>
> *~Grandma L. Levine*

6

are old enough to reproduce and we're old enough to have grandchildren, but emotionally we find ourselves asking, "How can I be a grandparent when I don't even feel like a grown-up?"

By adding a branch to the family tree, our children are giving us the perfect opportunity to reinvent ourselves once again as we sign on for the best job in the world. It's only that age thing we can't quite figure out.

The truth is that many people become grandparents at a very young age. Obviously, we're in that group. Besides, there's a sweet inevitability about taking this next step, so let's go for it and enjoy the show. In our hearts we know that age is only relative. And grandchildren are the best kind of relatives to have.

Fasten your seat belts. Next stop: Grandparentland.

Quiz No. 1: Grandparents on TV

Test your knowledge of classic TV characters and the actors
and actresses who played some of them.

1. Who portrayed Grandpa McCoy on *The Real McCoys?*
   a. Walter Pidgeon
   b. Richard Crenna
   c. Walter Brennan
   d. Leo G. Carroll

2. Who was the grandmotherly babysitter on *I Love Lucy?*
   a. Mrs. Stonehaven
   b. Miss Appleby
   c. Mrs. Trumbull
   d. Mrs. MacGillicuddy

3. Which actress was Granny on *The Beverly Hillbillies?*
   a. Irene Ryan
   b. Nancy Kulp
   c. June Lockhart
   d. Vivian Vance

4. What was the profession of Beaver's elderly friend, Gus,
   on *Leave It to Beaver?*
   a. Mail carrier
   b. Fireman
   c. Gardener
   d. Policeman

5. Who was Tabitha's grandmother on *Bewitched?*
   a. Clara
   b. Esmeralda
   c. Alice
   d. Endora

6. Who played grandfatherly *Marcus Welby, M.D.?*
   a. Fess Parker
   b. Robert Young
   c. E. G. Marshall
   d. Robert Ryan

7. Who was the house-keeping granddad on *My Three Sons?*
   a. Bub
   b. Billy
   c. Old Dad
   d. Scooter

8. Who portrayed Grandpa and Grandma Walton?
   a. Buddy Ebsen and Joan Bennett
   b. John McIntire and Jeanette Nolan
   c. Eddie Albert and Eva Gabor
   d. Will Geer and Ellen Corby

9. Name the actor who played Grandpa on *The Munsters.*
   a. Fred Gwynne
   b. Jackie Coogan
   c. Al Lewis
   d. Hans Conreid

10. If Little Joe had fathered a child on *Bonanza,* which character would the youngster have called "Grandpa"?
    a. Buck Cannon
    b. Lucas McCain
    c. Roy Coffee
    d. Ben Cartwright

Chapter 2
Let's Go Shopping

♫My mama told me, you better shop around.♫

~Berry Gordy and William "Smokey" Robinson

Even if it's the big news you've been waiting breathlessly to hear, learning of your impending leap into grandparenthood tends to be an unnerving experience. As if somebody just hammered the final nail into the coffin of your middle age. Was the Summer of Love really so long ago?

Don't be surprised if the glad tidings leave you both elated and depressed. It's enough to make you think about getting a tattoo or piercing some hidden body part. Anything to make you feel younger than a grandparent.

Now, calm down and step away from the tattoo parlor. Body art? Who do you think you are, Britney Spears or Kobe Bryant?

If you're an expectant grandmother, there's only one sure way to spell relief:

S-H-O-P-P-I-N-G

Not for yourself, but for that soon-to-be cutest, brightest, sweetest, and funniest grandchild in all the world.

If you're an expectant grandfather and shopping isn't your bag, you can still participate by toting the parcels around the mall and doing your best to keep the prenatal spending spree from swallowing up your life savings.

Before you and your credit cards head to BabyGap and the discount stores, take some time to clean out your closets and cupboards. You need ample room for the mountain of stuff you'll want to bring home in preparation for all the wee one's visits and baby sleepovers.

So toss out the mood rings, those once-adored Pet Rocks, your faded smiley-face plastic drinking glasses, and the Veg-O-Matic that turned slicing and dicing into an art form. You can sell the lava lamps on eBay. They've attained some retro chic, but they're not really your style anymore.

What about the CB radio? Out. The Betamax? Dump it, along with anything else in the house that isn't digital. You can't have your grandchild thinking you don't know what's what.

After you get the hang of it, it's easy to deep-six the pink Princess phone, instamatic camera, and your entire collection of eight-track tapes, plus the black-velvet Elvis painting that marked a major lapse in judgment during one best-forgotten seventies Vegas weekend.

Send your polyester shirts and leisure suits to the Smithsonian, but hang on to the puka shells and gold chains. Puka shells have a habit of going in and out of style, and gold is, well, GOLD.

Unless you have a Texas zip code, it's time to round up those cowboy hats and Tony Lama boots. You know, the ones you haven't worn since "Mamas Don't Let Your Babies Grow Up To Be Cowboys" topped the country chart.

Ready, Set, Shop

When you're primed to hit the stores, prepare to feel out of date and uninformed regarding all the essentials for twenty-first century youngsters. Fortunately, babies themselves are exactly the way you remember them. They still arrive with the same standard equipment and deluxe sound system they've always had. What's different is all the extra stuff that babies—and, therefore, grandparents—require these days. Watch out for some strange new terminology.

The enclosure you knew as a playpen is now a play yard, and it comes with its own rooftop terrace changing station. You might think a baby travel system is a website for infants who want to see the world, but it's just a fancy baby stroller that magically converts into a car seat. While you're at it, pick up a bouncer, a swing, a jumper, and a gym. These are all must-haves, along with the singing potty chair. Yes, really.

Speaking of furniture, you'll want a high-style high chair and a crib, plus all the crib accessories. (Designer baby sheets are optional, depending on how the budget's holding up.)

What about a baby bath center? It's only a plastic tub, so there's no assembly required. Don't forget the rubber duckies.

You can never have too many bibs, baby sleepers (with and without feet), sippy cups, and rattles, plus a Binky in every room. Studies have shown that these pacifiers work wonders for grandparents, too. You'll also need a supply of baby powders, lotions, creams, and shampoos. And diapers, a truckload of diapers.

14

 You'll discover lots of changes when it comes to baby toys as well because playtime has become too valuable to spend merely on fun nowadays. Even babies play to learn. They're on the fast track to advanced placement as soon as they can string together a couple of "goos" and "gaas."

Look closely at today's cute and cuddly toys, and you'll discover that many are tiny tutors in disguise. So babies can push, pull, and tap their way to wisdom when they get tired of just crawling around. A, B, C. 1, 2, 3. Red, blue, green. Baby Mensa here they come.

 Start your toy shopping with plenty of mirrored, textured, stacking, and linking toys, which have been specially designed to stimulate developing minds. No way is your drooling dumpling going to be left behind.

Toss in some of those high-brow names, too. Like the complete collection of Classical Baby DVDs and a Mozart Magic Cube. And remember, today's baby simply cannot hold his head up in public if he doesn't have his very own learning laptop.

When it comes to keeping your grandchild from harm, common sense is still your best friend, but you'll want to invest in outlet covers, a baby monitor, and a safety gate or two. Those childproof thingamajigs for drawers and cabinets will keep little hands from exploring in all the wrong places. They'll also discourage late-night snacks for grandparents who should be watching their waistlines.

You'll quickly learn that being a grandparent means never having to say you're sorry to a sales clerk or checkout counter display. You might as well attach a sticker to your forehead:

I'LL BUY ANYTHING FOR MY GRANDCHILD.

Why are those adorable outfits and toys, silky-soft stuffed animals, and clever gadgets so hard to resist? Maybe it's the grandparent magnets those crafty manufacturers hide inside.

If you're worried that all these expenditures might derail your retirement plans, just think about the many grandparental perks to offset trudging in to work every week. Like story-time cuddles, gap-toothed grins, shared confidences, and the absolute pleasure of being with a child you can return at the end of the day.

To say nothing of the tens of thousands of rewards points you'll be racking up on your Visa and American Express cards. The stores, the banks, and our nation's economy will love you for it. Ka-ching!

Dear Gamma and Gampa,

If you want my advice, just buy one of everything. You know I'm worth it. Here are a few ideas to get you started:

**Love you already,
Your Future
First Grandchild**

Puzzle No. 1: Sold!

TV commercials have always influenced our shopping decisions. Fill in the product names for these commercial slogans that originated in the fifties, sixties, and seventies. Then unscramble the letters in the shaded squares for the puzzle's master answer.

Across

4 Fly the friendly skies.

7 See the U.S.A. in your _____.

8 Sorry, Charlie.

10 Please, don't squeeze the ____.

11 Stronger than dirt.

Down

1 Two, two, two mints in one.

2 Kills bugs dead.

3 Have it your way. (2 words)

5 The San Francisco treat. (hyph. word)

6 Look, Ma, no cavities.

9 Takes a licking and keeps on ticking.

Master Clue

9Lives' finicky mascot (3 words)

Chapter 3
Picking a Name

♫ *Shirley, Shirley bo Birley*
Bonana fanna fo Firley
Fee fy mo Mirley, Shirley! ♫

~Lincoln Chase and Shirley Elliston

Granny Gidget? Grampa Opie? Our old favorites from *The Mickey Mouse Club* now meeska-mooska transformed into mousekegrandparents? Suddenly, it seems like all the TV kids we grew up with are becoming grandmas and grandpas. They're taking on fun nicknames as part of the role, and we can do the same.

That's right, it's not only that bouncing bundle of joy who receives a shiny new name these days. Grandpa and Grandma Boomer are donning catchy monikers, too. Why wait to see what the little tyke comes up with when you can choose your own name and coach your grandchild to say it just like she learns to say "Mommy" and "Daddy"?

Here are some possibilities to get you started. Use the blank space to write in a few ideas of your own.

If you lean toward the more traditional, you might want a grandma or grandpa alias that reflects your heritage, such as Tita or Tito (Spanish), Obaasan or Ojiisan (Japanese), Bibi or Babu (East African), Bubbe or Zayde (or any of their many spelling variations from Yiddish), Oma or Opa (German and Dutch). In parts of India, children call their mother's parents Dida and Dadu, while Swedish kids refer to their father's parents as Farmor and Farfar. No matter how near or far, endearing names help bring grandparents and grandchildren closer.

Keep in mind when you select your grandparental handle that you'll be hearing it for a very long time in a great many places. Don't saddle yourself with a name you wouldn't want shouted across a crowded playground. ("Help, Poop-Poop, help. Caitlin's hogging the slide.") Or down the cereal aisle in the A&P. ("No, Boobie. We want Cocoa Puffs, not Shredded Wheat.")

Choose a name that will be easy for your grandchild to say. For instance, Grammarammadingdong might sound cute in some bizarre supercalifragilisticexpialidocious kind of way, but that kid will be out of training pants before he can string all those syllables together. Better shorten it to Grammy or Gram. You soon-to-be granddads, don't try to recapture your youthful vigor with a name like Studpop when Dandy and Popdoodle have such a nice manly ring.

Watch out for dueling grandmas, a situation that occurs when both grandmothers want to adopt the same name. You can solve this problem by staging a quick winner-take-all game of *Family Feud.* Or simply attach first names to the disputed grandname, such as Mama Kate and Mama Linda. That way, nobody even has to think about kissing Richard Dawson.

Often step-grandparents enter the picture, presenting name challenges and identity crises of their own. Your grandchild might even feel less fortunate with only four people to call *Gran* and *Grandy* when many of her friends have six or eight. Talk about an extended family.

Long before the birth, you can test-drive your nickname by planting yourself in front of the expectant mother whenever possible. Make up a story or sit down for a cozy chat.

"Hello in there, Baby Joshua or Madison. It's me, Gammy. Can't wait to watch *The Andy Griffith Show* and *Green Acres* with you on TV Land."

GRANECDOTE
What's in a Name?

"When my grandson, Wyatt, was three years old, he was the youngest child in his neighborhood and none of the other children wanted to play with him. One day, we were out in his front yard when an older boy rode by on his bicycle. 'Johnny, Johnny,' Wyatt called out to the boy, pulling me toward the sidewalk, apparently convinced that I could help him attract the playmates he desired. 'This is my best friend. Her name is Nana.'"

~Nancy "Nana" Burley Spokane, Washington

"Hey, Punkin. Big Daddy here. We're stopping by to say 'hi' on our way to the concert. It's the Crosby, Stills, and Nash *Off Our Rockers* tour. Someday I'll tell you about my buddy who had a friend whose brother was a roadie for Creedence Clearwater Revival. Or was it Three Dog Night? Anyway, I know you're gonna love classic rock."

Don't forget to run your new name by the woman with the big belly and swollen ankles, and be sure to include her in some of the conversations, too. What she needs right now is plenty of TLC, not the feeling that you see her as nothing more than the rocket launcher for your future grandchild. Remember, she can put an end to your tummy tête-à-têtes at the drop of a hat or the rise of a hormone.

If you're one of those boomers who's still in denial about being called by any name resembling Grandma or Grandpa, you can certainly train the child to use your first name. But imagine the embarrassment he'll suffer introducing you as Janice or William on Grandparents Day at preschool when all his pals are flanked by people they know as Grandmom and Grandpop.

The bond between grandparent and grandchild is one of life's strongest. With your personalized nickname, you'll stand out from everybody else in that little one's life. Isn't that just the way you want it?

Quiz No. 2: Name That Boomer

Test your knowledge of these famous and infamous baby boomers. (You can decide for yourself which are which.)

1. Who wrote *The Green Mile* and *Hearts in Atlantis?*
   a. Scott Turow
   b. James Patterson
   c. Stephen King
   d. Michael Connelly

2. Name the actress who appeared in *The Big Chill, Fatal Attraction,* and *101 Dalmations.*
   a. Sigourney Weaver
   b. Glenn Close
   c. Susan Sarandon
   d. Jessica Lange

3. Who gained fame as the junk bond king?
   a. Donald Trump
   b. Michael Ovitz
   c. Michael Milken
   d. Paul Allen

4. Who directed *Splash, Apollo 13,* and *A Beautiful Mind?*
   a. Ron Howard
   b. Joel Coen
   c. Rob Reiner
   d. John Sayles

5. Who is the voice of Marge Simpson?
   a. Nancy Cartwright
   b. Rita Rudner
   c. Candice Bergen
   d. Julie Kavner

6. Which rock star was born Vincent Damon Furnier?
   a. Tom Petty
   b. Alice Cooper
   c. David Lee Roth
   d. Gregg Allman

7. Name the actor who appeared in *Pulp Fiction, Unbreakable, and The Negotiator.*
   a. Danny Glover
   b. Dennis Quaid
   c. Samuel L. Jackson
   d. Richard Gere

8. Who became a disco diva with hits including "Love To Love You, Baby" and "Last Dance"?
   a. Gloria Gaynor
   b. Donna Summer
   c. Chaka Khan
   d. Yvonne Elliman

9. Which journalist was the face of CNN for the Gulf War?
   a. Brian Williams
   b. Connie Chung
   c. Wolf Blitzer
   d. Greta Van Susteren

10. Who created the comic strip *Calvin and Hobbes?*
    a. Bill Watterson
    b. Gary Larson
    c. Cathy Guisewite
    d. Berkeley Breathed

Chapter 4
Waiting Game: Where's a Stork When You Need One?

♫*Anticipation, anticipation
Is making me late
Is keeping me waiting.*♫

~*Carly Simon*

ou've stocked up on baby supplies and infant toys. You've selected a snappy new nickname. Now what? You're ready for the fun to begin, but there's no way to expedite this special delivery.

It's like that edge-of-your-seat excitement you felt decades ago, waiting with your friends in a crowded auditorium for Santana or The Supremes to appear. Then somebody walked up on stage to announce that their bus broke down ten miles out of town. Major bummer. Unfortunately, clapping your hands and stomping your feet won't hasten your grandchild's arrival either.

While the recipient of your growing baby love is waiting in the wings, be sure you prepare yourself to take on the mantle of grampy- or grammyhood. Fellow boomers are resetting the bar for excellence in grandparenting, and it's up to you to keep the standards high.

First, here's a simple formula to obtain your personal BGFQ or Boomer Grandparent Fitness Quotient. Remember how much energy it took to be a parent? Multiply that amount by fifty, divide by the square root of your current age, then subtract the number of hours you put in as a couch potato every day. The answer is your BGFQ, your ideal energy level for grandparenting. You need to be in tip-top shape to maintain it.

So if your fitness program went out with your discarded ThighMaster and Jane Fonda VHS workout tapes, better grab your yoga mat or start hitting the gym STAT. And keep the heating pad and Bengay handy.

Next, let's determine your BGHQ or Boomer Grandparent Hipness Quotient. This is the true test of your cross-generational cool and ability to relate to your grandchild. Built-in boomer cool can only carry you so far, so it's essential that you keep up on all the new stuff, too.

GRANDMA KNOWS
Being a Grandparent Changes Everything

"I can't remember life before my granddaughter was here. I've become totally unconcerned about how I appear to the world if something I can do will bring a smile to her face."

~Chris "Grandma" Lehr
Fuquay Varina, No. Carolina

WHAT'S YOUR BOOMER GRANDPARENT HIPNESS QUOTIENT (BGHQ)?

For each question, circle Yes, No, or WC for Who cares?

1. Did you perform a death-defying act today besides getting out of bed in the morning?	Yes	No	WC
2. Do you know what color Barney is?	Yes	No	WC
3. Can you download songs to an iPod without asking anybody for help?	Yes	No	WC
4. Is your TV bigger than 36 inches?	Yes	No	WC
5. Can you name two Zac Efron movies?	Yes	No	WC
6. Have you made a call using Skype?	Yes	No	WC
7. Have you ever ridden a Segway?	Yes	No	WC
8. Can you name at least two of Dora the Explorer's sidekicks?	Yes	No	WC
9. Do you think of Black Eyed Peas as something other than food?	Yes	No	WC
10. Do you own a Bluetooth headset?	Yes	No	WC

Bonus questions:

11. Did you skateboard or go snowboarding in the past six weeks?	Yes	No	WC
12. Do you know the lyrics to even one Alicia Keys song?	Yes	No	WC
13. Can you name all The Wiggles?	Yes	No	WC

Scoring:

For the first 10 questions, give yourself 10 points for every Yes answer, 0 if you answered No, and 5 points for Who cares? (After all, healthy disdain is part of being hip.) Add 25 points each if you answered Yes to any of the bonus questions, then check the table below to see how you rate.

Your Score	What It Means	How To Improve In Nine Months or Less
90 +	Either you're super hip or you're lying.	No improvement necessary. Why not share your hipness secrets with less fortunate boomers? You'll be doing them and their grandkids a big favor.
70-89	You're right on track.	Keep up the good work. You might even boost your score by sprinkling your conversations with expressions like OMG, BTW, IRL, and TMI.
50-69	More than halfway there.	Buy some Ray-Bans, start your own blog, tune in to Noggin and Nick Jr., and see your BGHQ soar.
30-49	You might still have a chance.	Until your grandchild is due, spend every evening connecting with members of your posse on your BlackBerry while playing World of Warcraft on your laptop. During the weekends, watch plenty of MTV2, tossing cool phrases at the TV screen like "That's so sick." and "Swee-eet."

Your Score	What It Means	How To Improve In Nine Months or Less
10-29	Desperately seeking hipness.	There's only one possible course of action. Call the nearest skydiving school and make your first jump next week, wearing an OutKast T-shirt under your jumpsuit. As you descend, switch on your Droid's MP3 function and sing along with anything by Justin Timberlake. Just be sure you pull the cord before the final chorus. That's the boomer spirit!
0-9	Your BGHQ went AWOL.	For those grandparents-to-be who are truly hipness-challenged, diversionary tactics are your last hope. Start learning several awesome magic tricks today. Kids love them. Then get a lifetime pass to the nearest IMAX theater and maybe, just maybe, your grandchild won't notice how hopelessly unhip you really are.

"They don't call me Supergramps for nothing."

Looking for more ways to boost your BGHQ? Review some of the boomer-era biggies on the left. Then check to be sure you know who or what's similarly big today, as noted on the right.

Hip/Happening Then	Hip/Happening Now
Patty Hearst	Paris Hilton
Peyton Place	Wisteria Lane
Cars with fins	Cars with Wi-Fi
Handshakes	Fist bumps
Elizabeth Taylor and Richard Burton	Brangelina
Lily Tomlin	Tina Fey
Sock hops	Raves
Willie Mays	Derek Jeter
"Heeere's Johnny."	Conan, Dave, Jimmy, Jay
Julia Child	Rachael Ray

Besides taking a wild stab at getting in shape and working to bring your hipness level up to speed, what else can you do to channel those achingly strong feelings of love that start taking hold of you months before your grandchild is born?

There's always crib assembling and rocking chair staining for expectant grandpas, bootie knitting and quilt making for expectant grandmas. But grandparents have been doing those things since before they invented Pablum.

Start today acquiring every type of action figure you can get your hands on. Old or new. The more you find, the better. Because nothing is too good for your future grandson. By the time he's old enough to have an interest in such things, you'll have quite the collection, making him the envy of his friends. And making you one of his early heroes.

"I LOVE YOU"

Or be the first in your crowd to learn baby sign language. Then you can teach it to the expectant parents, too. That'll be a great way to communicate with Baby Taylor until she learns to talk.

Jot down all the funny childhood stories you can remember about the father- or mother-to-be. Little Andrew will love hearing about the day his dad got in trouble for putting a worm in Aunt Julie's lunchbox or how his mom had to sit on the naughty step because she said a bad word. (No need to divulge the word.)

This pre-baby period is also good for getting in touch with your inner boomer, the one who hasn't quite adjusted to the notion that you're really old enough to be a grandparent. Don't be too hard on yourself if you've still got a bit of that *Why me?* thing going. It's natural. But, rest assured, you'll forget all about it the minute you lay eyes on your grandchild.

In the meantime, brush up on your patty-cake and peekaboo, and that stork will be coming in for a landing before you know it.

Quiz No. 3:
Those TV Words We Couldn't Wait To Hear

Match the catch phrases with their vintage television shows.

1. My little goombah.

a. Rawhide

2. Stifle yourself.

b. Maude

3. Who loves ya, baby?

c. The Flip Wilson Show

4. What you see is what you get.

d. Sonny and Cher

5. Head 'em up, move 'em out.

e. Laugh-In

6. Sock it to me.

f. The Outer Limits

7. Ohhhh, Rob.

g. Kojak

8. God'll get you for that, Walter.

h. All in the Family

9. Mom always liked you best.

i. Dick Van Dyke Show

10. There is nothing wrong with your television set.

j. The Smothers Brothers Comedy Hour

38

Chapter 5
Congratulations. It's a Grandchild!

♫ *Good morning, starshine. The earth says hello.*♫
~Galt MacDermot, James Rado, and Gerome Ragni

merican humorist, television host, and grandfather Sam Levenson wasn't just playing around when he advised, "The simplest toy, one which even the youngest child can operate, is called a grandparent." If you think this won't apply to you, think again after that pint-sized operator has you firmly wrapped around one chubby little finger.

Seeing your grandchild for the first time is one of those moments that will be etched in your memory forever. Like the day you first heard "Hey Jude," the weekend you saw *The Graduate*, or the summer you read *The Catcher in the Rye*. Only this event is a hundred times more awe-inspiring than the other three put together.

Priorities change when you have a grandchild. All those things in your life that seemed so absolutely, earth-shakingly important before can't begin to compete with her button nose or his expressive eyes. To say nothing of that new-baby smell that grandmas in particular tend to find irresistible.

So whether it's pink or blue balloons tied to the new parents' mailbox, you won't need sixty seconds to see that this bundle of joy is the most amazing creature the universe has ever known. (At least since Mr. Spock arrived with his Vulcan mind meld.)

Once you hear those first few gurgles and coos, you'll pack your bags for relocation to Grandparentland. The place where tots are tops and "no" seems to disappear from your vocabulary.

GRANECDOTE
Coming Out of The Man Cave

"Being a grandpa has changed me from macho man to mush, and I love it. I never thought I could be this way. It's like I turned into a woman."

~No-Name Grampy

Now that there's a grandchild in your life, you can tell Charles Dickens all about great expectations. You wouldn't be a genuine grandparent if you didn't envision incredible things ahead for the newbie in the family.

If it's a boy, you see a combination of Superman, Iron Man, and Indiana Jones. Or if it's a girl, you're thinking Wonder Woman, The Bionic Woman, and all those Disney princesses rolled into one.

Maybe he'll become a movie star or a mover and shaker in the business world. Maybe she'll grow up to be an artist or discover a cure for the common cold.

Your grandchild could be the last contestant standing on *American Idol* circa 2035 or the first of a new generation to sit on the Supreme Court. She might . . . He could . . . What if . . . ? Do you think . . . ?

Whoa, Granny. Hold on a minute, Gramps. There's plenty of time for your grandchild to reach the Who's Who of Whatever. But right now that dimpled darling has exactly two things on his or her mind: "Feed/change/hold me." and "For heaven's sake, let me sleep."

While you contemplate the future, don't be surprised to discover that your grandchild possesses some unusual powers in the present. Like the way that pink-bootied cutie with the petal-soft skin makes your heart do a flip-flop whenever she's near. Or how you find yourself skipping the weekly poker game or canceling your manicure if it means spending extra time with the rosy-cheeked charmer in the blue corduroy overalls.

There's no fighting it. Don't even try.

When your grandchild starts to crawl, you'll be on the floor like an eager puppy, seizing any opportunity to see eye-to-eye with this most precious of playmates. Who says you can't teach an old boomer new tricks? Better amp up your fitness program.

Spoiler Alert!

Yeah, yeah, yeah. All that sentimental hopes-and-dreams baby stuff is great, and your offspring's offspring is bound to be one

impressive youngster. But keep in mind that every kid has a morning meltdown or an afternoon tantrum now and then. Your grandchild will be no exception.

In the blink of an eye, that formerly perfect Natalie can become a crying, screaming, red-faced monster. Or sometimes Baby Brandon will be so disagreeable, you'll think you've landed in a double feature of *The Good, the Bad and the Ugly* and *The Longest Day*.

Not to worry. Just exercise the Grandparent Escape Clause and return the offending party to the parents. It's such sweet revenge for everything your child put you through growing up.

Besides, grandkids are the ultimate reward for surviving parenthood and the real reason you let your own kids live when they were teenagers. So it's only fair that, where your grandchild is concerned, you experience mostly the good. Let the parents deal with the bad and the ugly.

As sure as Carol Burnett's earlobe tug sent a personal "Hello, I'm doing fine" message to her grandmother every week, children and their grandparents have a special connection unlike any other. Lucky you with both a starring role and a front-row seat as the story of your grandchild's life unfolds.

LIGHTS. CAMERA. ACTION.

The Ten Best Things About Being a Grandparent

1. Acting like a kid again and nobody thinks anything of it.
2. Singing silly songs.
3. Swapping baby anecdotes with your friends.
4. Smiling for no particular reason.
5. Revisiting all your favorite animated movies.
6. Knowing somebody who hasn't heard any of your jokes.
7. Starting a new Hot Wheels collection.
8. Displaying the latest generation of refrigerator art.
9. Receiving spontaneous hugs.
10. Sharing all that love.

Puzzle No. 2: One, Two, Buckle My Shoe

How well do you remember some of the best-loved nursery rhymes? Fill in the individual answers, then unscramble the letters in the shaded squares for the puzzle's master answer.

Across

   3 Tuffet-sitting little miss

   5 Ran away with the spoon

   7 He met Simple Simon

   9 Twice the piper's son (2 words)

 10 Mary, Mary was quite this

 11 That faraway twinkler

Down

   1 Bo Peep lost them

   2 Those three vision-impaired rodents (2 words)

   4 Wall-sitter's first name

   6 Corner-sitter's last name

   8 Girl with a little lamb

Master Clue

This one climbed up the water spout (3 words)

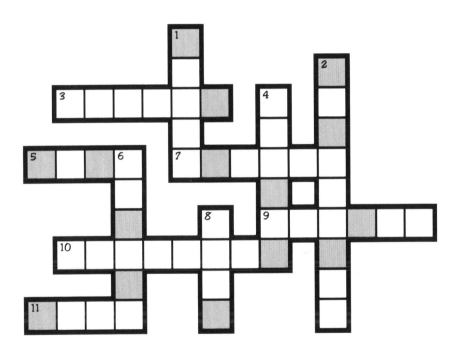

45

Chapter 6
Oh, Baby, How Times Have Changed

♫ *What happened to the world we knew*
When we would dream and scheme
And while the time away
Yester-me yester-you yesterday.♫

~Ron Miller and Bryan Wells

asn't it only yesterday we baby boomers were the new kids on the block? Now our grandkids are entering a world nearly unrecognizable from the one into which we were born. It's enough to blow your mind.

Long before car seats became an essential part of every baby's kit and caboodle, boomer newborns rode home from the hospital cradled in our mother's arms. Once inside the house, Mommy carried us past the entertainment center in the living room: a Philco console TV, an RCA Victor phonograph whose needle alternately skipped and got stuck, and a modest collection of scratchy 78 rpm records.

Then she took us by the communication system, Ma Bell's rotary dial telephone, on the table in the hall. Beyond that was the nursery, where the most sophisticated piece of equipment was the night light on the dresser. There wasn't a baby monitor or nanny cam in sight.

Daddy captured our first black-and-white smiles on a Brownie box camera and was even known for a time as the neighborhood king of home movies, thanks to his 8 mm camera and projector. Sadly, friends and even relatives eventually started making themselves scarce the

minute he suggested setting up the screen. We boomers were cute, but how many times can you expect people to watch the same kids ride trikes in the driveway or smear frosting on their faces at a birthday party?

A Tech Tale, Part 1

Got our first PC or Mac
And a cell phone way, way back,
But there's so much that we lack
Toward being tech heads.

Email, pay bills, surf the Net.
Book some travel? Sure, you bet.
Basic phone calls, no text yet
'Cause we're not tech heads.

We hear iThis, then iThat.
They say try this, then try that.
These gizmos are where it's at,
But we're not tech heads.

Technology progressed considerably by the time we had our children, but today things are advancing so quickly that our often digitally challenged boomer brains find it hard to keep up in a world overrun with electronics.

Fortunately, our grandchildren are coming along at the ideal time to help us with the gadgets we already have and the new ones that seem to appear every day.

In one of life's greatest mysteries, today's kids are somehow born with a built-in tech gene. They're multitasking at two and downloading personalized ringtones before they're even allowed to cross the street on their own. We boomers couldn't imagine

> ## A Tech Tale, Part 2
>
> *Got the big HDTV,*
> *Tivo, too, and DVD.*
> *They can work so easily*
> *If you're a tech head.*
>
> *Got a zillion channels and*
> *All these movies on demand.*
> *We try to be in command,*
> *But we're not tech heads.*
>
> *More remotes than we could need,*
> *All with buttons we can't read.*
> *Help us make them work, we plead.*
> *We're so not tech heads.*

a time without a phone for every home, but these kids can't imagine a time without a cell phone for every person.

Soon we'll hear that scientists have discovered a way to insert retractable baby earbuds that grow right along with the child, so Jayden and Emma can be wired in from day one. That'll make for one lengthy call-waiting period before they're able to say "hello."

THEN	NOW
Baby blocks	Baby blogs
Carbon paper	Carbon footprint
Parents saving for college	Parents saving for preschool
The $64,000 Question	Who Wants To Be a Millionaire?
Caroline and John-John	Malia and Sasha
"I apologize."	"My bad."
Father Knows Best	Oprah knows better
Lickable photo corners	Digital photo files
Curl up with a good book	Curl up with Kindle
When I'm Sixty-Four: whimsical song	When I'm sixty-four: reality

It's not only technological breakthroughs that affect us boomers as we continue our journey from "Oh, What a Night" to "Those Were the Days." So many of the things we thought would always be with us have simply faded away.

> ## A Tech Tale, Part 3
>
> *Got ourselves an MP3.*
> *Can we download tunes? Let's see.*
> *Where, oh, where's the USB?*
> *We're just not tech heads.*
>
> *Figured out the playlist now,*
> *Lots of oldies, goodies. Wow!*
> *Not so hard when you know how.*
> *Oh, to be tech heads.*
>
> *Love to listen all day through.*
> *Boomer songs, it's déjà vu.*
> *We could swap some songs with you*
> *If you were tech heads.*

We get nostalgic for old-time jukeboxes, slow-dancing to "You've Lost That Lovin' Feelin'" and "Cherish," and singing along with lyrics you could actually hear over the music.

What became of the Doublemint twins, the Frito Bandito, and those beautiful Breck girls? Did they run off with Bucky Beaver, the intrepid mascot for that long-ago Ipana toothpaste?

When was the last time you were inside a phone booth or even passed one on the corner? Forget about reaching that nice lady who used to give us the correct time no matter when we called. She's gone on to that great switchboard in the sky.

Some of our old hangouts, like A&W and Dairy Queen, updated themselves for the twenty-first century, but we miss real soda fountains and drive-ins with pony-tailed carhops. We want to return to our friendly Woolworth's five and dime and the lunch counter that served cherry pie as good as Grandma used to make.

Big things keep changing, too. We grew up secure in the knowledge that there were nine true planets revolving around the sun. Then, out of the blue, Pluto got demoted. Well, that's just goofy. What's next? A recessionary Saturn having to pawn some of its rings or face exile to another galaxy?

For better or worse, many of the food products we knew and loved as children remain on the market half a lifetime later. Wonder Bread, Twinkies, and Spam survived, along with Eggos, Velveeta, and Oscar Mayer Wieners. Cracker Jack is still around but, alas, they don't make prizes like they used to.

A Tech Tale, Part 4

Got a camera, so advanced.
Digital, all fancy pants.
Can we work it? Not a chance.
We're still not tech heads.

Then came grandkids and we knew
Our tech-fearing days were through.
Can't miss kiddie pics. Could you?
We must be tech heads.

So we've learned to upload fast,
Photo sharing's such a blast.
We have seen the light at last
And we are tech heads.

Breakfast cereals have shown amazing longevity, so we can share some of our childhood favorites with the grandkids. Like Trix and Frosted Flakes, Cheerios and Sugar Crisp (the one dentists prefer two to one). Rice Krispies are still with us, too, but it's harder for us to hear the old snap/crackle/pop these days. Rumor has it that the research team at Kellogg's is exploring ways to turn up the volume for its longtime boomer consumers.

We see child-rearing philosophies changing as today's kids experience fewer spankings and more timeouts. They're not expected to be good every single minute.

When we were kids, questioning parental authority bought us a one-way ticket to our room—end of discussion. As parents, we taught our children that their opinions counted, and we gave them some say in their young lives. No doubt, our kids will give their kids even more latitude, and we'll be the ones tsk-tsking in the background. And so it goes.

Yes, now that we're grandparents, it seems as if just about everything's different from the way it used to be. Except babies, especially when they're your very own grandchildren, remain the sweetest of creatures. Maybe, when you think about it, things are really changing for the better.

Puzzle No. 3: Some Things Never Change

These children's favorites have stood the test of time. Fill in the individual answers, then unscramble the letters in the shaded squares to form the puzzle's master answer.

Across

2 Earthy desserts (2 words)

5 Theodore Roosevelt's namesake (2 words)

8 That little spinner

10 Draw a picture with colorful hands

11 It floats on the wind and you hold the string

Down

1 Peanut butter partner

3 Grinch creator (2 words)

4 Tinkerbell's buddy (2 words)

6 Flavored ice on a stick

7 You take the Xes, I'll take the Os (hyph. word)

9 "You're it!" game

Master Clue

Little red wagon (2 words)

55

Chapter 7
Baby Steps: There's a First Time for Everything

*♫ Yesterday a child came out to wonder
Caught a dragonfly inside a jar.♫*

~Joni Mitchell

very grandchild arrives with an endless list of potential firsts to be lovingly noted, and duly checked off, by doting grandparents. Even the oh-so-mellow boomers can be ruthless when it comes to measuring our grandchildren's milestones against those of our friends' grandkids.

♥ Baby Matthew rolled over in his crib. **Check.**

♥ Emily ate two spoonfuls of strained peas. **Check, check.**

♥ Little Gavin's hair is finally coming in. **Check it out.**

♥ Maya was all smiles for her Santa photo op. **Checking it twice.**

♥ The twins are starting to walk. That's **checkmate.** At least as far as any low-lying objects in your townhome are concerned.

For successful grandboasting, the key is in revealing only those details that paint your grandchild—and, by association, you—in the best light.

For instance, there's no need to mention the dozen spoonfuls of strained peas the dog lapped up from the kitchen floor before Emily decided to try some. Or how those toddling twins wiped out two orchid plants, put a dent in your walnut coffee table, and did serious damage to a trio of Limoges boxes during last week's visit.

Be on the lookout for any mega-milestones, which you have to share with your friends immediately. Like when that precocious Elijah points right at you and utters something that resembles "grr-um-ph," but which you might exaggerate ever so slightly in the retelling into a nearly crystal-clear version of "Grandpa" or "Grandma."

You'll want to bring up the fun smaller accomplishments, too, such as brilliant young Zoe beating you at Cootie or assembling a whole Mr. Potato Head on her own.

58

What to do when another grandparent emails all your friends about three-year-old Alexander's recent encounter with his first onion ring at

Applebee's? You simply click on "Reply All" and tell your tale of exiting Denny's

the other day with four-year-old Isabella, who sashayed past each booth and table on her way to the door. This diva-in-training wasn't leaving before she got a smile or wave from every other patron in the place.

With today's cell-phone video capabilities, a friend can capture his darling granddaughter and her playmates splashing around in an alligator-shaped inflatable pool and broadcast the show to an extensive network of grandparents in seconds. Be prepared to fire right back with the latest footage from the petting zoo, featuring your cute *and* fearless grandson getting up close and personal with a lamb.

If you're among the truly technologically inclined grannies and grampies, think of all the granecdotes you can Twitter to your friends and other followers to document your grandkids' exploits.

- ♥ Nicholas has been diaper-free for a week and gladly pulls his pants down to prove it. **Tweet.**

- ♥ Sarah, that angel, went right down for her nap. Now Nana can watch *All My Children.* **Tweet dreams.**

- ♥ Sanjay's finger painting looks a lot like an early Picasso. **Abstract tweet.**

- ♥ The twins were ecstatic this morning when they spotted the baby robins in the elm tree. **Tweet-tweet.**

- ♥ Mackenzie is the most adorable Snow White ever. Sending photos tomorrow. **Twick or Tweet.**

- ♥ I'm one proud Grandpop! Logan recited the entire alphabet this morning. **A-B-C-Tweet-E-F-G.**

And that's only the beginning because these brag-worthy firsts never stop. Multiply by two or three or more as additional grandchildren join the family, and you'll have miles of milestones stretching out before you. Maybe one day you can simply press a button to teleport yourself and your grandchild to your friends' homes for impromptu sessions of Show and Tell.

Of course, you'll compare your grandchild's progress with that of your own offspring, the child's parent, as well. While you're babysitting that cute Rachel, you might turn to your spouse and ask, "Wasn't Junior starting to walk about this age, honey? It was right after those bikers moved into the apartment next door." or "Remember how we hung on every syllable before our little Susie said her first actual word? We couldn't wait to hear 'ma-ma' or 'da-da.' Then she simply said 'kitty.'"

Ten Exciting Firsts for Grandparents

1. You see your son's eyes in your granddaughter's face.
2. Enrique gets a tooth.
3. Riley stays overnight.
4. Your grandson picks you a flower.
5. Noah calls you Mom-Mom.
6. Enrique loses a tooth.
7. Owen tells you a secret.
8. Riley goes home after staying overnight.
9. Brianna asks you to kiss her boo-boo.
10. Holding each grandchild for the very first time.

Everybody knows that babies have to crawl before they can walk. Grandpas and grandmas go through quite a learning process of our own as our grandchildren progress from infancy and toddlerhood through the tween years and beyond.

We boomers thought we were pretty squared away raising our kids, but it's been a long time since we navigated that bumpy road. Now we're at a new starting line as grandparents. We'll take some wrong turns and plenty of detours as we go because being a grandparent is totally different from being a parent.

You don't have all the responsibility except when you sometimes do. It isn't a full-time gig except when it occasionally is. And nobody wants your advice except on the days when they ask. So you're constantly walking a tightrope between do/say too much and do/say too little.

To help you on your grandparenting way, here are the three most important things for you to remember. Make them your mantras and recite each several times a day.

Mantra #1

My child is every bit as capable of good parenting as I was.
(Heaven help us.)

Mantra #2

Better to stuff a cookie in my mouth than give unsolicited advice.
(Make that chocolate chip.)

Mantra #3

I may have strong opinions, but it doesn't mean I'm always right.
(Pffft!)

First smiles. First hugs. First words. Enjoy them while you can in that initial delirium of new grandparenthood, when you feel as if the smallest thing your darling Hailey or Michael does is nothing short of perfection.

Then you can start over again each time a new grandchild arrives.

All too soon, however, grandkids are talking back, acting defiant, and blurting out embarrassing words at the most awkward moments. That's when you realize they're only human, just like you.

Except when they turn into teenagers and you wonder if they've changed into a different species altogether. But that's another story.

Puzzle No. 4: Baby-Boomer Firsts in History

Provide the last name of the first boomer to attain the position or achievement in each clue. In some cases, he or she was also the first or only person ever to reach that pinnacle. After you complete the individual answers, unscramble the letters in the shaded squares for the puzzle's master answer.

Across

4 Jane became a *Today Show* anchor.

6 George was heavyweight champ before firing up the grill.

7 Tom took home back-to-back Oscars.

8 Garry's strip earned a Pulitzer Prize for editorial cartooning.

11 Chris won six French Open singles titles.

Down

1 Sally was the first American woman in space.

2 Nancy was the LPGA's top rookie and player in the same year.

3 Dan grew up to be the U.S. VP.

5 Terry was the winning quarterback in four Super Bowls.

9 Condoleezza became secretary of state.

10 Patty didn't need a miracle to be an Oscar recipient at sixteen.

Master Clue

Winner of 22 Grammy Awards for male solo artist (2 words)

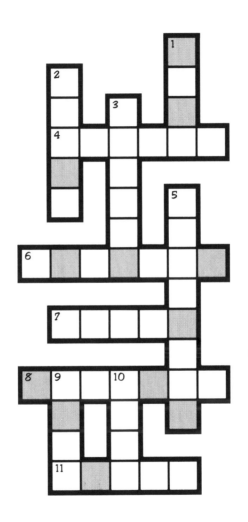

65

Chapter 8
Grandparentland: What a Trip!

♫*Joy to the world*
All the boys and girls, now
Joy to the fishes in the deep blue sea
Joy to you and me.♫

~Hoyt Axton

n Grandparentland, streets are paved with unconditional love, and grandchildren always seem to have the right of way. It's as if these little guys and gals were putting up kid-friendly road signs that compel us to do their bidding.

STOP
for
Häagen-Dazs
when
grandchildren
are present

GO
DIRECTLY TO
McDONALD'S FOR
HAPPY MEALS
(ONLY PLAYLAND
LOCATIONS,
PLEASE)

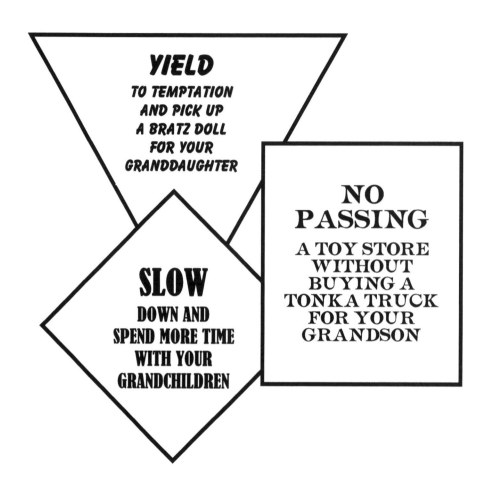

YIELD
TO TEMPTATION
AND PICK UP
A BRATZ DOLL
FOR YOUR
GRANDDAUGHTER

NO PASSING
A TOY STORE
WITHOUT
BUYING A
TONKA TRUCK
FOR YOUR
GRANDSON

SLOW
DOWN AND
SPEND MORE TIME
WITH YOUR
GRANDCHILDREN

This isn't one of those exotic locales we envisioned for ourselves as we cranked up Led Zeppelin on the stereo or played all those beer-drinking games in our misbegotten younger days. But now that we're here, we're settling in nicely while retaining a healthy level of boomer cool. When we stop to recall our own grandparents and how we saw them when we were kids, the contrasts are mind-boggling.

THEN	NOW
Grandpa drove an Oldsmobile.	Grandpa rides a Harley.
Grandma wore housedresses and orthopedic shoes.	Grandma wears capris and sassy sandals to show off her pedicure.
Grampy had an old cane.	Grampy has a new knee.
Gran and Gramps took a cruise, and the grandkids got to hear all about it.	Gran and her partner take a cruise, and the grandkids get to go with them.
Grammy knit sweaters for everybody.	Grammy buys everybody gift cards.
Grandpa swore at the TV and adjusted the rabbit ears.	Grandpa swears at the TV, cable box, remote, and Grandma.
Nana baked everything from scratch and never heard of "me time."	Nana frequents the cakes and cookies aisle at Costco and takes herself to the spa.
Granddad stored his teeth in the medicine cabinet at night.	Granddad stores his Viagra in the medicine cabinet day and night.
Grandma went to bridge club.	Grandma goes to book club and pilates.
The grandkids loved spending time with Gran and Gramps.	The grandkids love spending time with Gran, her second husband, Gramps, and his new girlfriend.

Along the highways and byways of Grandparentland, we're discovering a very different landscape right in our own back yard. Where we used to have eyes only for the newest sports bar or Italian restaurant, home improvement stores, art galleries, or kitschy second-hand shops, now we're scoping out tot lots, puppet shows, and ceramics classes for children.

Parks and playgrounds are our new stomping grounds, where there's nothing more entertaining than watching Dylan and Olivia on the climbing equipment or pushing Connor in the swing. It's a natural high.

Just as Chutes and Ladders is our new favorite game, we're cheering from lawn chairs at soccer practice and looking on with amazement as kids run the bases in the wrong direction during T-ball. (Yes, sometimes there *is* crying in baseball.)

70

One day, we're attending a post-game pizza party, the next day a preschool graduation.

Numbered among the many fringe benefits for citizens of Grandparentland are free tours by the people who know the territory best: our grandkids. For instance, if you have trouble navigating all the ins and outs of a Build-A-Bear Workshop, your grandchildren will be happy to assist you. Naturally they get to keep any bears you create.

Or if you're new to water parks, they'll gladly show you around each splish-splashing attraction, drenching you at every opportunity. Look out for those cannonballs.

Grandkids know what's up at the multiplex concession stand, too. Not only will your little sweeties introduce you to that fabulous offer known as "the kids' combo," but they'll show you how fast they can make it disappear. Then everybody will need to visit the restroom just in time for the climactic scene of the movie, and you'll never know how it all turned out. So much for happy endings.

> ## GRANECDOTE
> ### Wake-Up Call
>
> *"My three-year-old grandson just loves to scream. When I visit, he'll come screaming down the hall in the morning and fling open the guest room door. 'Parker, what are you screaming about?' I ask. He says, 'I love you, Grandma,' throws himself on the bed and gives me a hug. How do you argue with that?"*
>
> *~Grandma Patty*
> *Burbank, California*

Quiz No. 4: The Grandparentland Permit Exam

Have you got what it takes to be a good grandparent? Here's a simple test to earn your official Grandparentland Permit.

1. Where in the world is Grandparentland?
   a. Florida
   b. California
   c. Hawaii
   d. Wherever you happen to be

2. What's the best answer when your grandchild asks about the birds and bees?
   a. "It all starts when a boy bee meets a girl bee . . ."
   b. "First, the two birds build a nest . . ."
   c. "Let me pull out my PowerPoint presentation."
   d. "Ask your parents."

3. Who are the biggest VIPs in Grandparentland?
   a. The grandparents with the most grandkids
   b. The grandparents with the most money
   c. You and all your friends
   d. Your grandchildren

4. If your grandchild asks your age, how should you respond?
   a. "Younger than all your friends' grandparents."
   b. "Younger than that redwood tree."
   c. "Count your fingers and toes, then add a little more."
   d. "Sorry, I didn't hear the question."

5. What's the one and only law of Grandparentland?
   a. Grandchildren should be seen and not heard.
   b. Everything goes better with a martini.
   c. Grandparents are always right.
   d. Have a blast.

Taking up residence in Grandparentland is like setting sail on your own special edition of *The Love Boat.* Except now you're Captain Stubing and your grandkids are Julie, Gopher, and Isaac,

 who are constantly getting into mischief and need your gentle guidance to stay on a smooth course.

Since these youngsters are a generation once removed, you can maintain the easygoing attitude with them that you wouldn't have dreamed of showing toward their parents when they were growing up. Even so, grandkids alternately delight and exasperate you because it's their job to ensure that nothing goes as planned when they're part of the equation.

Fortunately, what your grandchildren lack in consistency, they make up for in adorableness, which they can pull out of their pockets like fairy dust and sprinkle

wherever it's needed. Research indicates this mystery substance is more potent in Grandparentland than anywhere else on earth, particularly when it's paired with bad behavior. So try not to laugh, even if they misbehave in the cutest ways, because grandkids are very quick to learn what their Nana and Pops will and won't let them get away with.

In fact the stay-young-forever baby boomers are the most laid-back grandpas and grandmas in history. In other words, we're a whole lotta fun.

That's good news for our grandkids, which makes them want to spend more time in Grandparentland. And when they want to spend more time in Grandparentland, that's good news for us.

You'll find countless rewards in this happy place, but there are some sacrifices, too, beginning with those not-so-subtle changes in your home and lifestyle. Can you dig it?

Say Goodbye To	Say Hello To
A tidy house with pristine furnishings	Ketchup-stained sofa cushions and fingerprints on the walls
Stimulating conversations with your grown children about politics and philosophy	Endless monologues by your grandkids' parents about breast-feeding and new child-rearing techniques
Romantic wine-and-cheese evenings for two	Boisterous Chuck E. Cheese's evenings for too many
Lace-trimmed towels in the guest bathroom	Mud-streaked towels all over the place
Colorful language	Ixnay on the adbay ordsway
Linen tablecloths	Plastic placemats
Eagles and Chicago reunion concerts with your friends	*Shrek* and *Scooby-Doo* DVDs with your grandkids
Chocolate soufflé by candlelight	Cotton candy by the merry-go-round
Tooling around in your red sports car	Loading kids' car seats into your gray sedan
Privacy, peace, and quiet	Grandparentland Central Station

Chapter 9
Fun 'n' Games

♫*It went Zip when it moved and Bop when it stopped*
Whirr when it stood still
I never knew just what it was and I guess I never will.♫

~Tom Paxton

uying kiddie toys, games, and other gear is one of the pleasures of being a grandparent. Just ask the junior executives at Mattel, Hasbro, and Toys "R" Us, who are banking their early retirement on it.

The problem is we're bombarded with so many choices that it's nearly impossible to know what to select. And no matter how carefully you weigh the options, these kids will be into something new next week, thanks to the nonstop marketing that turns them into unquenchable consumers while they're only little squirts.

We're talking board games, video games, musical toys, magical toys, tiny cars, tiny trains, kiddie boats, kiddie totes, books to read, dolls to feed, toys that walk, toys that talk. And on and on.

Add endless TV and movie tie-ins, and you've got enough loot to fill every home in America five times over. Soon children won't be sleeping in beds anymore. They'll simply carve out space to lay their heads amid all their wall-to-wall stuff.

As we contemplate this dizzying array, we can't help looking back fondly on the modest selection that satisfied our young needs. Our toys ran on imagination and sheer kid power. They never needed rebooting. That was something we did in the winter, along with remittening, before we went outside to play.

Our bedroom floors were the original play stations, perfect for an afternoon game of Candy Land, Slapjack, or Sorry! Who needed technology when we could build the strangest contraptions with Tinkertoys or an entire town out of Lincoln Logs? Of course, we took it for granted that kneeling and sitting cross-legged on the floor were part of our body's repertoire then.

Being a child was a lot less complicated in the age of *The Flintstones* and five-cent candy bars. When we weren't in school, Mom and Dad were happy to have us play and play. It kept us out of their hair during a time when parenting wasn't the frantic, all-encompassing activity it is now.

We filled the hours with marbles and yoyos, jump ropes and jacks. We picked up sticks, acted silly with putty, and got tiddly with some winks in our day. Boomer kids fell hard when hula hoops arrived, especially those of us who could spin one around our waist and another around our neck simultaneously. Surely nothing could ever top that.

THEN	NOW
Toys to wind up	Games to download
Howdy Doody	Hello Kitty
Shari Lewis and Lamb Chop on TV	Elmo Live
Roller skates that attach to your shoes	Roller shoes
"Buy me a pony."	"Buy me an Xbox and a pony."
Rocky and Bullwinkle	SpongeBob and Patrick
Roy Rogers lunch pails	Hannah Montana backpacks
Jump your opponent in checkers	Jump to the next level in Super Mario
Popeye	Pokémon
Lions and tigers and bears. Oh, my!	Decepticons and Romulans and Green Goblin. OH, MY!

Quiz No. 5: It's All in the Games

Test your knowledge of these classic games
you'll love playing with your grandchildren.

1. Who was NOT a suspect in the original Clue game?
   a. Colonel Mustard
   b. Mrs. Black
   c. Mr. Green
   d. Miss Scarlet

2. To successfully "shoot the moon" in Hearts, the tricks you
   take must include all 13 hearts and which other card?
   a. King of diamonds
   b. Queen of spades
   c. Ace of clubs
   d. Deuce of clubs

3. Bamboo, flower, and wind tiles are used in which game?
   a. Mancala
   b. Parcheesi
   c. Go
   d. Mahjong

4. What color are the Monopoly properties Marvin Gardens
   and Atlantic Avenue?
   a. Red
   b. Blue
   c. Yellow
   d. Green

5. Infantry and cavalry pieces are part of which game?
   a. Stratego
   b. Risk
   c. Backgammon
   d. Mille Bornes

6. Q and Z are worth how many points each in Scrabble?
   a. 8
   b. 15
   c. 10
   d. 5

7. When you win at regular solitaire, also known as Klondike, which cards top each of the four piles?
   a. Jacks
   b. Nines
   c. Kings
   d. Aces

8. The star-shaped board for Chinese Checkers has how many points?
   a. 5
   b. 6
   c. 7
   d. 8

9. Which chess piece can only move diagonally?
   a. Knight
   b. Queen
   c. Rook
   d. Bishop

10. What is the secondary name of the Barbie board game?
    a. Adventures in Fashion
    b. A Date with Ken
    c. Dress for Success
    d. Queen of the Prom

Now that those no-tech times are only a memory and the so-tech times are here to stay, childhood is a whole different ballgame. But that doesn't mean you have to fill your grandkids' toy chest with nothing but electronic wonders.

Many long-ago favorites are still on the market or just waiting up in the attic to be rediscovered. Why not introduce your grandkids to one of the oldies for every new-fangled item you buy? That way, the kids will benefit from the latest playtime technology and you'll savor watching them enjoy some of the toys and games you and their parents remember so well.

If Colin craves action figures, give him Transformers, G.I. Joe, and Halo toys. Then bring out your trusty old toy soldiers, and who knows what's in store?

Since Anna loves to be on the move, you can't go wrong with a new razor scooter. When she's ready to slow down, introduce her to your vintage kaleidoscope.

Indulge Akira's passion for video games by buying him Need for Speed. Later, you can dust off your old basketball and show him how to execute a crossover dribble.

GRANDPA KNOWS

"The more time you spend with your grandkids, the more they love you in return and feel safe to just be themselves. When I'm with my two grandsons, we play whatever make-believe games they want to play, even if it means becoming Robin to their Batman and Superman."

~Duffy "Papa" Clark
Orange, California

Help the twins learn about earlier eras by giving each an American Girl doll. Once they master braiding the dolls' hair, it's time to teach them to play cat's cradle with a single piece of string. Guaranteed to produce matching ear-to-ear smiles.

You can also bond with your grandkids over Internet versions of some of the games you used to love, like hangman, Yahtzee, and Battleship. No need to shake your laptop when you want to erase that online Etch A Sketch, however. A couple of keystrokes and you can start again from scratch.

Mother May I?

It's great to surprise your grandchildren with special gifts from time to time, but don't be catching their parents off-guard. Check with them *before* you buy. Although you raised one of them, Mommy and Daddy have their own ideas about the toys and games they want their progeny exposed to.

If only our childhood View-Masters had allowed us to see into the future, we would've been blown away by the evolution of toys and games that was on its way. As we watched the 3D exploits of Zorro and Mighty Mouse, we never imagined that our grandkids' fun would center around a remote control, a palm-sized rodent, or a keyboard of buttons to tap.

Old and new generations. Old and new ways to play.

Chapter 10
You've Come a Long Way, Granny

There you are one day, innocently applying mascara at your lighted magnifying mirror, when it finally—inevitably—hits home: that woman looking back at you has logged a lot of decades. Yep, you really have reached the grandmother time of life.

Once your children have children, it's hard to fool even yourself into thinking you're still young because sixty only feels like the new forty when you're not standing next to an actual forty-year-old who's already discovered the wonders of Botox.

But what's a bit of sagging here and there, a laugh line or ten between you and your grandchildren? When Baby Ethan wakes up from his nap and sees your smiling face, he's not counting the crow's feet. While you give freckle-faced Chloe her bath, she isn't judging you for having skin that pooches more than hers. (Okay, maybe they count and judge a little, but it's only out of curiosity.)

In your grandkids' world, you're the poster child of grandmas because you're *their* grandma. So you can let yourself age naturally or become a glam gram with your own extreme makeover. They don't care. You're simply Mimi or Nonny to them.

They'll get a kick out of hearing how life was when you were a child. You know, in the Dark Ages.

Remember racing home from school every day to see which couples were dancing on *American Bandstand?* Arlene and Kenny were sooo cute. Show your grandkids how you could do The Stroll and Mashed Potato with the best of them.

Did you giggle with your girlfriends over the lingerie pages in the Sears catalog? So many unmentionables all in one place. Thankfully, those horrendous girdles you marveled at went out of fashion before you had much that needed holding in.

What happened to your gum-wrapper chain and the autograph book you had everybody sign? You got some real gems.

```
  2 GOOD
+ 2 BE
  4 GOTTEN
```
MY ♥ ∧ 4 U

And they think txt msgs and emoticons are revolutionary.

Baby-Boomer Grandmas Remember When:

➤ Putting pin curls or rollers in your hair was a nightly ritual.

➤ Fifty cents an hour was the going rate for babysitting. (Now you gladly do it for free.)

➤ Thongs were something you wore on your feet.

➤ Audrey Hepburn was the epitome of elegance.

➤ A transistor radio was your most prized possession.

➤ You had to wait for a Sadie Hawkins dance to ask a boy out.

➤ "It's snowing down south" was a real wardrobe malfunction.

➤ Chunky platform shoes didn't seem like an accident waiting to happen.

➤ *Dr. Kildare* and *I Spy* were must-see TV.

➤ "The Little Old Lady from Pasadena" couldn't be you.

If you were a typical boomer girl, you probably had a pen pal or two, twirled the baton, read all the Nancy Drew mysteries, and imagined growing up to be Miss America so Bert Parks would sing his special song for you. How hard could it be to prance around a big stage in a bathing suit and high heels?

Tell your grandkids how you took piano lessons or played clarinet in the school band just like they do now. Which was smart thinking in case the Miss America thing panned out and your baton-twirling talents were lacking.

You couldn't decide which one you were more in love with, so you carved all four names into your notebook:

JOHN   GEORGE

PAUL   RINGO

Plus the initials of that cuter-than-cute guy who sat behind you in science class. Then you wrote all about him in your diary.

Dreaming of That Happily Ever After

Back then, being a grandma someday was the furthest thing from your mind, but you couldn't wait to turn eighteen. You knew that was when all the secrets of the universe would be revealed and your life would become as perfect as a Doris Day/Rock Hudson movie.

In the meantime, you stocked up on Clearasil and Yardley lip gloss and sneaked peeks at your mother's copies of *The Group* and *Lady Chatterley's Lover.* You spent hours poring over the latest fan magazines and trying everything you could to look more like Colleen Corby or Cybill Shepherd in *Seventeen.*

One day you sold Girl Scout cookies door-to-door. The next day you were going steady with a boy whose hair was longer than yours. Mom and Dad had a fit when you brought him home.

Your boots were definitely made for walkin', and your adventurous spirit was eager to tag along. But coming of age as a boomer was like marching to the beat of two different drummers at the same time.

One side of you was all good-girl innocence, firmly entrenched in your parents' traditional values. But the other side was ready to experience flower power, free love, and everything else the alluring new counterculture brought your way.

Your closet was a showcase of the many facets of you, running the gamut from Twiggy's Carnaby Street mod look to the frenetic San Francisco style of Janis Joplin and Grace Slick. It featured mini-skirts and maxi-coats, peasant dresses long and short, pantsuits, hot pants, T-shirts, cutoffs, and—the mainstay you wore most of the time—those authentic indigo-blue jeans from the Army-Navy Surplus store.

Through the years, you had a huge assortment of TV role models. First, it was those never-desperate, ever-in-a-shirtwaist-and-pumps perfect housewives like June Cleaver. Then it was the feisty, independent gals such as *That Girl* and Emma Peel of *The Avengers.* But it was WJM's own Mary Richards who made you feel as if you really could turn the world on with a smile.

Once you started reading *The Feminine Mystique, Fear of Flying,* and *Ms. Magazine,* things would never be the same. Boomer women stood up for themselves at work and sat down to dinner with their families every night. You proved that you could have it all and found it both exhilarating and exhausting to do so.

Grandma, What Big Changes You've Made

One thing's for sure: boomer grandmas are nothing like your own grandmas, who smelled of lavender and Ivory soap and kept a cloth handkerchief tucked up their sleeve. They darned socks, canned peaches, and never came close to being cool. You wouldn't have wanted them any other way.

You'd find them in the kitchen most of the time, where they doled out fresh-baked goodies and sage advice in equal measure. "Don't wish your life away," one of your apron-clad grannies might exclaim as she pulled a tray of heavenly cinnamon rolls out of the oven. "Summer vacation will be here soon enough."

90

Or "If you don't have anything nice to say, don't say anything at all," your other grandma would scold when you made disparaging remarks about friends or siblings while helping her stir the fudge.

Barely seeming scoff-worthy then, these pearls of wisdom are now among the life lessons you want to pass on to your grandkids, along with brushing their teeth in a circular motion.

Boomer women are light-years beyond the generations of grandmas that came before. Today's grannies are running marathons and companies. Some nanas are staying home, and others are flying into space. And you can cook up new enterprises as effortlessly as you cook up a meal.

True, your days of cutting out Katy Keene paper dolls and slipping Fabian's picture under your pillow each night are in the past. You're wearing granny glasses for real now and, whoops, was that another hot flash? (Open freezer door, insert head.)

But you identify as much with the women of *Sex and the City* as you do with *The Golden Girls*. And, while it may seem as if you've gone from blue jean baby to the Red Hat Society in no time at all, you've still got it and it's getting better every day.

So forget the rocking chair. Place your order without delay for that personalized license plate you've been thinking about. You know the one: HOTGRMA. You go, girl.

Puzzle No. 5: Ooh, What a Dreamboat

Provide the last names of these teen idols who made boomer girls swoon. Once you fill in all the squares, unscramble the letters in the shaded squares for the puzzle's master answer.

Across

3 Peter was Herman to the Hermits.

4 Rod had strong feelings for "Maggie May."

7 Troy starred with Sandra Dee in *A Summer Place*.

8 Sam's mega-hits included "You Send Me" and "Chain Gang."

9 Paul portrayed Donna Reed's TV son.

Down

1 Davy was the only British member of The Monkees.

2 Steven was inspired to "Dream On."

3 Ricky was a "Travelin' Man."

5 Frankie frolicked at the beach with Annette.

6 Chubby gave our lives a twist.

8 David played a Partridge.

Master Clue

The undisputed king of teen idols. (2 words)

Chapter 11
The ABCs of Grandparenting: Who's Teaching Whom?

♫Don't know much about algebra
Don't know what a slide rule is for
But I know that one and one is two
And if this one could be with you
What a wonderful world this would be.♫

~Sam Cooke, Herb Alpert, and Lou Adler

IF you think there's a generation gap between you and your children, there must be at least a generation Grand Canyon between you and your grandchildren. But that's part of what gives us such a strong connection with these chips off the chips off the old block. Our life experiences and scope of knowledge are so far removed from theirs that we can learn a lot from each other.

You can tell your grandkids about be-ins and love-ins, and they can tell you about the flash mob they saw at the plaza. Mob? Oh, dear. Was anybody injured? No, they assure you. It's just for fun. Everybody wore blue, and they were dancing. Look, here's the cell phone video we took.

Anytime these in-the-know guys and gals throw unfamiliar lingo your way, such as *chillax, frenemy,* or *check my vitals,* you can share vintage expressions like *hang loose, neato,* and *catch you on the flip side.* They all make equal sense. Or no sense at all.

Ten Things You Can Learn from Your Grandchildren (If You Don't Already Know)

1. The most recent adventures of Captain Underpants.

2. Why you haven't seen one of today's animated or action movies until you've seen it in 3D.

3. How to cram half a dozen pieces of Bazooka Bubble Gum in your mouth at a time.

4. Rock-scissors-paper is still a great way to settle a dispute.

5. Why Taylor's rise has been so swift.

6. How to play Crazy Old Fish War.

7. You can be totally loved even with morning bedhead.

8. Sometimes the box it came in is far more interesting than the most carefully selected gift.

9. How to make grape juice come out of your nose.

10. You're never too old to try something new. (Maybe too stiff, tired, or out of shape, but never too old.)

Calling English 911!

With the current state of English, one of the most important things you can teach your grandchildren is how to use the language well. Experts tell us it's in transition, but that's just a polite way of saying it's going to hell in a handbasket.

WE USED TO HEAR:	NOW PEOPLE SAY:
Hello.	Dude.
Is everything all right?	Dude?
Oh, that's terrible.	Duuude!

And that's only the tip of the linguistic iceberg. Let's assess the overall damage, which seems to get worse every day:

➢ **GRAMMAR:** A lot of folks don't talk so good.

➢ **SUBJECT AND VERB AGREEMENT:** Those nouns and verbs is frequently out of sync.

➢ **SPELLING ERRORS:** Rampunt.

➢ **SYNTAX:** Huh?

➢ **WORD USAGE:** Bad. Except when bad sometimes means good. But you never know when that applies. Which makes it bad. Or is that good?

Part of the problem is the ever-increasing body of knowledge we're asking the human brain to accommodate nowadays. Our grandchildren are soaking up information about a million times faster than we ever did, but they must have a zillion times more to learn.

These youngsters are under tremendous pressure to be on the road to success at an early age, but nobody expected us to start planning for AP classes while we were still watching *Romper Room* or *Ding Dong School.* Our parents thought we were doing fine as long as we could write our names and read "See Spot run" in first grade.

Imagine what clever boomers could've accomplished by that age if Mom and Dad had motivated us as much as parents do today. Or if one of those mammoth UNIVACs hadn't weighed in at something like 29,000 pounds. That was nobody's personal computer and not even close to being user-friendly.

Today, little Caleb and Sophia are beginning to read, write, and find their way around cyberspace at the unbelievably early age of three or four. This raises the question: Are they amazing because they're our grandkids or are they our grandkids because they're amazing? Either way, these apples of our eye don't fall far from the family tree.

Long before technology took its place as both subject matter and teaching method, boomers

studied what American kids had been learning right along: your basic English, history, geography, science, and math. Add a dash of art and music, a foreign language, home ec for the girls and shop class for the boys, and that seemed to be everything we needed to know.

Of course there were  those unexpected blips on the curriculum radar. Like when they rolled out *New Math.* What was up with that? Some odd thing about base-7, where 10 came right after 6, leaving 7, 8, and 9 out in the cold. Fortunately, it didn't stick. So now it's history.

We thought geography was a piece of cake until we grew up and started noticing all these countries rearranging themselves and taking on new names. Eventually we figured out that the map of the world

is a work in progress, but when we were kids we never dreamed what they taught us in school might one day stop being true.

THEN	NOW
Learn how to type	Learn how to input
The Emerald City	Hogwarts
Memorize your multiplication tables	Grab your calculator
My Friend Flicka	Photos of my friends on Flickr
The USSR	Russia, some other countries, and a bunch of Stans
Welcome Back, Kotter	Glee
"Look it up."	"Google it."
Pass a note in study hall	Text message during history
Put on some clothes and go to the library	Stay in your jammies and go to Wikipedia

What's a boomer to do with all the new words, concepts, media, machines, and cultural phenomena crossing our paths every day? If you want to stay on top of things, there's only one thing to do: talk to your grandchildren.

But don't expect them to spend all their free hours spoon-feeding you the latest and greatest. You'll have to soak up some information yourself. So keep those still-agile brain cells fully charged by playing chess, Scrabble, and occasional video games; working crosswords and Sudokus; and frequently tuning in to *Jeopardy* or, at the least, watching *Are You Smarter Than a 5th Grader?*

> ## GRANECDOTE
> ### Candid Camera
>
> *"When I showed some black and white photos from my childhood to my five-year-old grandson, he looked surprised, asking, 'Grammy, when did they invent color?' He thought the whole world must've been black and white back then."*
>
> *~Brenda "Grammy" Perrier*
> *Nashua, New Hampshire*

Maybe you've noticed the major shift in intergenerational interaction because so many boomer grandparents require child supervision when operating their tech toys. It's not that we're incapable of doing things on our own. But it's hard to remember how all these doohickeys work if we don't use them and their various functions every day. Plus, the whereabouts of their instruction manuals are anybody's guess.

Here's a typical conversation that recently took place between Gammy, age 60, and Aiden, age 7:

Sweetie, can you please help me add some new numbers to my cell phone?

SURE, GAM. OPEN UP YOUR MENU.

Menu? Oh, I get it. You want me to order pizza while we do this.

NO, GAM, THE MENU ON YOUR PHONE.

Oh. Why?

BECAUSE YOUR CONTACTS ARE IN THE MENU.

Why?

BECAUSE THAT'S WHERE YOU KEEP THEM.

Why?

SO YOU CAN CALL YOUR FRIENDS.

Why?

BECAUSE YOUR GRANDCHILD SAYS SO.

Like the many grandparents who came before us, we boomers have an abundance of know-how to share with our grandchildren. But these days it's obviously a two-way street. In a world that keeps advancing at breakneck speed, grandkids are the key to our continuing education. And don't they make the cutest teachers?

Quiz No. 6: The Plot Thickens

Maybe you forgot the end of the book you read last week, but how well do you remember the ones you read decades ago? Match the sixties and seventies fictional characters with the books that made them famous.

1. John Yossarian   a. Breakfast of Champions

2. Sissy Hankshaw   b. The Godfather

3. Kilgore Trout   c. Love Story

4. Atticus Finch   d. The Exorcist

5. Neely O'Hara   e. On the Road

6. Michael Corleone   f. Even Cowgirls Get the Blues

7. Jennifer Cavilleri   g. One Flew Over the Cuckoo's Nest

8. Sal Paradise   h. Catch-22

9. Regan MacNeil   i. Valley of the Dolls

10. Randle McMurphy   j. To Kill a Mockingbird

Chapter 12
The Grandkids Are Coming!
The Grandkids Are Coming!

♫ You look like an angel
Walk like an angel
Talk like an angel
But I got wise
You're the devil in disguise.♫

~Bill Giant, Bernie Baum, and Florence Kaye

e survived waterbeds, est seminars, *Jaws,* shag carpet, streakers, Boy George, and Y2K. Plus assorted midlife crises. But can boomers survive a few days alone with our grandkids?

When Mommy and Daddy are out of the picture on that much-needed weekend getaway, you don't have the option of giving the kids back following the evening's last game of Uno or after you polish off your morning oatmeal. They're suddenly no-deposit, no-return as you find yourself on the play date that never ends.

Of course you love spending time with your grandchildren, except you might be accustomed to experiencing their boundless energy and endless antics in slightly smaller doses. Such as afternoon excursions to the duck pond or Taco Night at the local Mexican restaurant.

But two or three whole days together? How quickly *The Brady Bunch* can become *The Dirty Dozen*, made even worse by the fact that Alice doesn't live there anymore and you have to do all the work. At least it's a labor of love.

 Try not to go bonkers in the first half hour, even when the grandkids turn your living room into Legoland or start racing from one end of the house to the other in a spontaneous simulation of the Indy 500. Above all, maintain a position of strength by establishing that you're the boss at the outset. Yeah, right. We all know who's really in charge in today's kid-centric world.

But everybody will act as if it isn't true. For example, your grandchildren will politely ask permission before hooking up their Wii to the television set in the den, and you'll pretend to weigh the decision carefully before giving your consent after they've already started their game.

Soon every flat surface in your previously home, sweet home will be covered with Game Boys, coloring books, barefoot dolls, a bead kit, Zhu Zhu Pets, a toy fire truck brigade, and a one-eyed

stuffed zebra that somebody will be crying for at bedtime.

As your surroundings start to resemble something out of *Mad Max* and the decibel level rises to that of a 747 flying directly overhead, take a few of those from-the-diaphragm deep breaths and remind yourself that this weekend, too, shall pass.

Things have certainly changed from the times we boomers spent with our grandparents, when they mostly left us to our own devices. Oh, sure, we sat on the front-porch swing with Grandpa reading *Beetle Bailey* and *Little Lulu* in the Sunday comics or searching the sky for shooting stars on a balmy summer night. And Grandma got us all together for three square meals a day. But our grandparents didn't feel they

GRANECDOTE
Power Play

"My wife, Judy, gave my grandson rules of the house when he came for a visit. 'No jumping on furniture, no running in hallways, no hands on walls.' Graham, then six, pondered this new equation for a minute and said, 'I've got one. How about no Judy?'"

~Rod "Grandpa" Vickery
Mission Viejo, California

had to entertain us every minute. They just went about their business, and we modified our routine to fit with theirs. Now we're doing it again—in reverse—and it gets a bit nerve-wracking.

What's for Dinner?

Inspired weekend meal planning is a must, so you can forget that unimaginative food pyramid the nutrition police advocate unless you want to hear the nonstop mealtime blues. Better get in tune with the Culinary Kiddos, a four-star panel of youngsters promoting common-sense cuisine. Here's what they recommend:

Cooking for Your Grandchildren
(It isn't rocket science.)

1. **The Protein Group:** Hot dogs, chicken nuggets, barbecued ribs (the messier the better), and peanut butter.

2. **Those Comforting Carbs:** Mac 'n' Cheese, SpaghettiOs, creamed corn, and Tater Tots.

3. **From the Dairy Case:** String cheese and chocolate milk.

4. **The Waffle Group:** Pancakes, French toast, waffles, and any other foods you can get kids to eat by covering them—the foods, not the kids—with syrup.

5. **The Dessert Tray:** Ice cream, ice cream cake, pie with ice cream, pie with cake. And don't forget the s'mores, the tasty treat that's been both food and event for about a hundred years.

Decorating some foods with faces or themes can make them more desirable for kids to eat, but never, ever try this with liver, tofu, or Brussels sprouts. Fido will be the sole beneficiary of these healthy foods because you can bet those little scamps will feed him every last morsel under the table. If you don't have a dog, for weeks afterwards you'll discover tiny tidbits in various stages of decay that were pocketed and later stashed all over the house.

Many granddads report excellent results with the sometimes controversial **Muncha Buncha Cruncha** group, which is the ideal accompaniment for watching sports with your grandkids on TV. While everybody chows down on Cheetos, potato chips, M&Ms, Oreos, and buttery microwave popcorn, you can explain the subtle differences between a curve ball and a slider or why a football team needs both wide receivers and a tight end.

For all you gammies and gampies who might feel guilty about letting your grandchildren go without veggies for a couple days: get a grip. It's not as if you were abandoning the kids on *Survivor* to forage for themselves. If the parents complain, remind them that it's a small price to pay for babysitting while they indulge in that kid-free R&R they've been dreaming about. Guilt can work both ways, you know.

With meal planning out of the way, be sure you have plenty of activities lined up for you and your grandkids to enjoy together.

Puzzle No. 6: Where To Go, What To Do

What were some of your favorite things to do and places to go when you were a child? Now you can revisit them with your grandchildren. Fill in the individual answers, then unscramble the letters in the shaded squares for the puzzle's master answer.

Across

2 Bull-riding, calf-roping, and barrel-racing

3 Go there for story time and all those wonderful books

4 A blanket, a basket of food, and here come the ants

6 Waves to splash in and sandcastles to build

9 Creating masterpieces from paper, glitter, crayons, and glue

10 Where you can hold a starfish and see the whale show

Down

1 Saddle up those little buckaroos (2 words)

3 The place to fish in summer and ice skate in winter

5 Blue-ribbon pigs, handmade quilts, and prize-winning 4-H exhibits (2 words)

7 Where you can watch your ship come in

8 Art, history, or science on display

Master Clue

The Number One destination for kids of all ages

111

Make household chores part of your grandchildren's weekend with you, too. The kids won't mind. They're already on a first-name basis with dirt.

Think weed-pulling in the garden, wiping down the baseboards, and removing all those dust bunnies that have been accumulating under the beds. It's character-building for them and means less bending over for you.

Anyway, these kids need to learn that being with Moomaw and Pampaw only means non-stop fun 99.99 percent of the time.

Ready for Some Relief?

Eventually, with all this togetherness, your mind and/or your energy will snap. That's when you introduce the grandparent-friendly games. Popular titles include "How Fast Can Everybody Pick Up the Mess?" and "Who Can Pretend To Be Asleep the Longest?" Or try the new advanced version, "Play Dead." They're self-explanatory, and you can make up the rules as you go along.

Or switch to Plan B. Simply hand over the TV remote (after ensuring the parental controls are in place) and tell the little hooligans to watch what they want for the rest of the visit.

GRANDMA KNOWS

"What happens at Grammy's stays at Grammy's."

~Colleen "Grammy" Rowe
Huntington Beach, California

When all else fails, when you've run out of patience—and margarita mix—dial 1-800-I-GIVE-UP. Now it's a job for the Child Whisperer, who offers the following free advice:

Five Sure-Fire Tips for a Successful Weekend with Your Grandkids

1. Forget about cleaning the house before they arrive so you won't feel bad when they turn it upside-down.

2. Don't play favorites; bribe each child to be good with an equal amount of cash.

3. Turn that lock every time you go into the bathroom because children never met a closed door they didn't want to open.

4. Remember that kids repeat everything they hear, and young ears hear everything.

5. Keep your blood pressure medication handy.

Have a Wonderful Time!

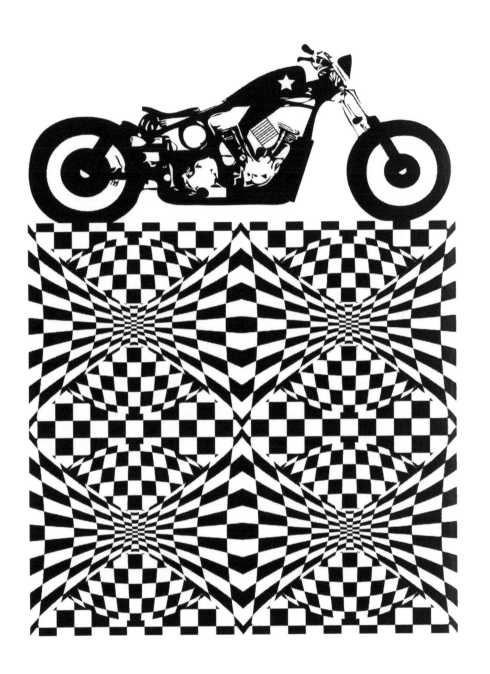

Chapter 13
He Ain't Heavy, He's My Grandpa

♫*Get your motor runnin'*
Head out on the highway
Lookin' for adventure
And whatever comes our way.♫

~Mars Bonfire

ey, Grandpa. Or do you prefer Daddums or Gampy? No matter what your grandkids call you, you've retained that boomer male mystique in plentiful supply. It's a quality that's not easily defined. Sort of a Duke of Earl/King of the Road/Pinball Wizard/Desperado kind of thing. And recently you've added old-guy wisdom to the mix.

So even if the beard's gone gray, something creaks every time you get up from the couch, and that extra room you need in your jeans these days is closer to a skosh and a half, you and your compadres are the grooviest grampies ever.

Grandchildren see it right away, which is why yours is the lap Hannah can't wait to sit on and your stories are the ones that have Liz and Max hanging on every word.

And if you can remove a quarter from their ears the way your grandfather used to do, your grandpa stock will soar higher than anything Wall Street has to offer.

Of course life isn't all hunky dory for boomer granddads. Sometimes you face major dilemmas.

Like how to watch the Super Bowl *and* attend the matinee performance of *Mary Poppins,* the musical, with your wife and grandkidlets, which you agreed to long before you gave any thought to the exact date of the gridiron spectacular. Uh-oh.

Or how on earth to answer an inquisitive preschooler's latest questions when there are no other grown-ups around to consult.

From the serious: "Poppy, is it ever okay to tell a lie?"

To the outrageous: "Gampa, why does Nana have those two round knobby things under her sweatshirt and you don't?"

Ten Ways To Know You Really Are a Grandpa

1. Can't stop making wacky faces over the crib (even after your grandchild falls asleep).

2. Now associate "We Will Rock You" with a baby and a warmed bottle.

3. Feel a little jealous when everybody says your grandchild looks like the other gramps.

4. Suddenly get the urge to whittle.

5. Regain your appreciation for Bugs Bunny, Daffy Duck, Sylvester, and Tweety.

6. Actually read the directions before assembling a new toy.

7. Have a desire to play cops and robbers again.

8. Want to share your philosophy of life with a four-year-old.

9. Replace your old lawn furniture with a new swing set.

10. Can't get that "Small World" tune out of your head.

Once you get used to the idea, being a grandfather seems as natural as constantly running and jumping did when you were a kid and hardly ever running and jumping does now.

Every moment you spend with a grandchild can be an amazing journey of rediscovery as you witness many of the day-to-day happenings you'd stopped noticing somewhere along the way. Follow a fuzzy caterpillar's progress up the driveway with your granddaughter or share your grandson's first wide-eyed look at falling snow, and you'll wonder what else you've been missing.

It makes you recall some of the pleasures of your boomer boyhood, such as Slinky, that genuine Davy Crockett imitation coonskin cap, and your Dick Tracy two-way wrist radio. And remember those imaginative structures you used to build with that Erector Set?

What's become of your old sci-fi toys, such as the plastic ray gun, the battery-operated robot, or the secret decoder ring? You thought by now you'd be flying around in a personal spaceship like they did on *The Jetsons.* Instead, you're stuck in the same old daily traffic jam right here on the ground.

You can still picture those lazy summer afternoons down at the creek, where you'd explore, swim, fish, and maybe catch a frog that would mysteriously wind up in your big sister's bed that evening. Or, if you were a city kid, you'd swim in somebody's backyard pool or the one at the park. Marco. Polo. Marco? Polo!

Later you'd participate in a monumental game of Monopoly on somebody's wraparound front porch. That know-it-all kid down the street would volunteer to be banker until the rest of you finally caught him palming gold five-hundred-dollar bills. If he's a real-life banker or CEO today, it's probably high time the big boys made him play truth or dare.

With Dad's push lawn mower or a paper route powered by your trusty Schwinn, you earned money to spend on baseball cards, comic books, and new stamps for your collection. All together, these treasures might be worth a small fortune today, but chances are they disappeared along with your model airplanes and the chemistry set that made your parents really glad they invested in that extra-large fire extinguisher.

Open Sesame

These days you've got a password just to open your list of passwords. But when you were a kid, you and the other boys only needed the one for gaining access into your treehouse club.

The club had one hard-and-fast rule:

NO GIRLS ALLOWED!

Except, of course, Tommy's mom, who made an occasional appearance to drop off tuna sandwiches, cookies, and a thermos of lemonade. The food was great, but what stays in your memory is how her Evening in Paris perfume lingered on the air after she climbed back down the wooden slats.

If you wanted a little solitude, you could hole up in your room

for hours captivated by *The Hardy Boys, The Black Stallion, Swiss Family Robinson,* or *The Call of the Wild.* You imagined yourself to be quite the adventurer. Then you went to camp, heard your first ghost story, and lay awake in the tent all night clutching your flashlight.

In your quest for TV heroes, those bland and often bumbling sitcom dads didn't make the cut. Although you wouldn't have minded trading places with Gilligan if it meant being marooned with either Ginger or Mary Ann.

Men of action like *The Lone Ranger* and *Sky King* were the ones you admired. You would've given anything to be as tough as Robert Stack on *The Untouchables,* smooth like James Garner on *Maverick,* and as cool under fire as James Arness on *Gunsmoke.*

Your hero at the movies had all these traits and more. The star of *Rio Bravo*, *The Man Who Shot Liberty Valance*, and *True Grit* himself: Marion Morrison, AKA the more rugged-sounding John Wayne.

Today's actors are inclined to use the names they were born with,

even those less-than-rugged, often unpronounceable ones. So when you go to the movies with your grandkids, you're rooting for the likes of Shia LaBeouf, Ashton Kutcher, and Orlando Bloom. What would Marion think about that?

How'd You Get To Be Such a Good Sport, Granddad?

Your lifelong passion for sports began long before round-the-clock programming on ESPN, Fox Sports, Versus, and all the others. Maybe it started on a dusty Little League field, where visions of becoming the next Sandy Koufax or Hank Aaron danced in your head. Or on a YMCA basketball court, where you imagined you were playing alongside Bill Russell and Wilt Chamberlain.

Then again, the simplest explanation is that it's an integral part of those male genes handed down from your father and his father. That's why you could never get enough of watching athletes such as Jim Brown, Jack Nicklaus, or Muhammad Ali do what they did so well.

If things didn't work out for you in the world of sports, you thought you could always become a rock star. That garage band you started might've been the next Beach Boys or Lovin' Spoonful, too, if your mother hadn't insisted on parking the new station wagon in the middle of your practice studio.

Whether you were the letterman's sweater and wingtips type or you wore a black leather jacket and boots, it wasn't easy navigating the rocky shores of adolescence. That's one of the few things that doesn't change from generation to generation, so be sure you're there for your grandkids when they reach the terrible teens. Sometimes it's easier to discuss their problems with a grandparent than a parent, especially if the problem *is* the parent.

Your One and Only

You'll never forget your first love and how your heart swelled with pride when you were out together. She was one souped-up baby, adorned with chrome rims and pinstripes. Let Dad have his four-door model; it was two-door or nothing for you.

Having your own set of wheels spelled freedom with a capital F. All you and your friends could think about were drive-in movies, cruising Main  Street on Friday nights, and spring break, here we come.

Fast-forward a bunch of decades and who knows how many road trips later, and it feels like you progressed from teendom to grampydom lightning quick. There's no way to apply the brakes now, so lean back in your La-Z-Boy and enjoy the ride.

Your strobe lights and psychedelic posters may be long gone, and you haven't worn bell bottoms or an Afro in ages. But when it comes to being right on, far out, and outta sight, that's one hat trick you can still pull off easily.

So what if you and your friends talk fiber content and sodium intake as frequently as you toss out baseball stats these days. Or if topics like prostate exams and colonoscopies have found their way into your halftime conversations.

Good grandpas stay on top of these things so they can stick around to become great grandpas and have lots of years with their grandkids.

Besides, you could use more time to figure out those still-confounding baby-boomer women.

Puzzle No. 7: Oh, Brother, That Guy Can Play

Millions of boomer boys dreamed of growing up to be a great athlete. Provide the last names of the ones in this puzzle who did. After you fill in the individual answers, unscramble the letters in the shaded squares for the puzzle's master answer.

Across

4 Kareem scored an NBA-high 38,387 career points.

6 Ray followed Olympic glory with 36 professional boxing wins.

9 Edwin cleared many hurdles to win Olympic gold four times.

10 Nolan threw 5,714 career strikeouts at the old ball game.

11 Mark wouldn't get out of the pool until he won nine Olympic gold medals.

12 Joe left his heart and four Super Bowl wins in San Francisco.

Down

1 Dick flopped on his way to revolutionizing the high jump.

2 Dale drove around and around to win 76 Winston Cup titles.

3 Reggie's slugging skills earned him five World Series championship rings.

5 Jimmy had quite a racket going with 160 consecutive weeks at Number 1.

7 Eric speed-skated to Olympic gold in five different events.

8 Golf suited Tom to a tee when he won eight majors.

Master Clue

ESPN named this younger boomer the top athlete of the 20th century. (2 words)

Chapter 14
Holidays + Grandchildren = Too Much Fun

♫ *Well, way up north where the air gets cold*
There's a tale about Christmas that you've all been told
And a real famous cat all dressed up in red
And he spends the whole year working out on his sled
It's the little Saint Nick.
It's the little Saint Nick.♫

~Brian Wilson and Mike Love

hether you deck the halls or observe other seasonal celebrations, there's nothing like grandkids to put the ho-ho-ho back in your holidays. Much of the magic went away when your children grew up and left home, but it returns like a custom-order boomerang as soon as you have grandchildren.

These cheery cherubs, who can brighten up any old day with their quirky questions and disarming smiles, give you a fresh perspective on the joys and wonders of this special time of year.

What could be better than unwrapping Lily's first clay handprint with the tiny chip that makes it more endearing? Or watching Jack attack a caramel apple minus his two front teeth?

Drive the grandkids around to look at decorations or lead them in a boisterous rendition of "The Chipmunk Song," and you'll be filled with memories of your childhood holidays.

Remember the best gift you received as a child? Perhaps it was that Mickey Mantle glove that brought you and your dad closer together or the Twister game that tried to pull everybody apart. Close your eyes and you can still hear the whistle of your Lionel train or the "Dance of the Sugar Plum Fairy" playing on your ballerina music box.

Funny how almost everything you wished for back then was different from the things you're hoping for now.

The Baby-Boomer Holiday Wish List

THEN	NOW
Ribbon candy and foil-covered chocolate coins	See's, nothing but See's
A bigger allowance	A bigger 401(k)
Higher grades	Lower cholesterol
Win the soapbox derby	Win the lottery
A shiny new bell for your bicycle	A shiny new car for your driveway
Cool shoes	Comfortable shoes
A backyard playhouse	An oceanfront estate
Stay up all night	Sleep through the night
Balcony seats for The Rolling Stones	Front row seats for The Rolling Stones
Grow up faster	Grow old slower

With the renewed holiday spirit that grandchildren bring to your life and the unique brand of merry mayhem today's youngsters can stir up, your seasonal activities as a grandparent could go something like this.

Getting Ready

Ask the smaller tykes to make ornaments for a special kids-only tree, and they'll probably provide felt snowmen, construction paper chains, and odd but interesting pipe-cleaner creatures.

Extend the same invitation to your tween-aged grandkids, and they'll come up with downloaded photos of Lady Gaga, Justin Bieber, and Beyoncé. Not quite what you had in mind, but it's their tree. And you have to applaud their ingenuity.

 Things probably won't be cookie-cutter perfect when the cutie-patooties help you with holiday baking either. After you convince them that clean hands make for better-tasting goodies, be on the lookout for big-nosed monsters or other non-holiday shapes they'll try to sneak onto the cookie sheets. Don't be surprised if everybody winds up in a giant flour fight long before the first batch of doughy angels, stars, snowflakes—and who knows what else—goes into the oven.

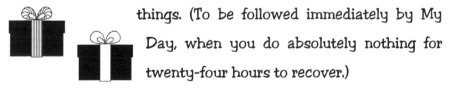Your grandchildren will love having their own holiday stockings at your house. When it's time to hang the personalized legwear on the mantel, grab the step-stool and your smallest hammer and confirm the whereabouts of the first aid kit. Uh-huh, you'll be the daredevil holding the nails with one hand as you guide the little boys' and girls' hammer strokes with the other. Don't think of it as a recipe for disaster. Think of it as the holiday way to start building their confidence with tools.

Giving and Receiving

Later, as you nurse that tender thumb, fill the stockings with sidewalk chalk, Matchbox toys, kazoos, crayons, sparkly barrettes, candy canes, and bottles of bubble blow.

Get creative with personalized gifts for your grandkids, like Kayla Day, when it'll be just you and Kayla doing her favorite things. (To be followed immediately by My Day, when you do absolutely nothing for twenty-four hours to recover.)

Almost as much fun as giving presents to your grandkids is seeing what they come up with for you, particularly if they make the gifts themselves.

Young Jacob will burst with excitement as he gives you his elbow macaroni picture of . . . Let's see, is it a cat, a tree, or his favorite character from *Sesame Street?* No matter who or what, you'll love it.

Sometimes your grandchildren's gifts have their own secret strategies. Like the spice jars Grace and Zachary decorate for you and fill with *their* favorite Jelly Bellies. Or the Fuddruckers gift certificate Daniel can't wait for you to open. He's confident you wouldn't think of asking anybody to accompany you there but him.

If you're lucky, you might get five-by-seven photos of Abigail and Addison, those exuberant red-headed twins, in matching frames they fashioned out of popsicle sticks. (Abby's the one on the ice.)

The Holiday Feast

All too many boomers live with the memory of being routinely banished to the children's table in the kitchen when holiday mealtime rolled around. Oh, the sense of rejection. But that's the ghost of holidays—and therapy sessions—past, and there's so much to celebrate in the present.

Now the kids get to sit at the big table with the grown-ups, and they put on quite a show.

The little ones shriek, crawl under the table, and claim not to be hungry while expertly smooshing potatoes, gravy, and cranberry sauce into a ghastly soup on their plates. Not five minutes later, they're dishing up big helpings of Jell-o salad.

The older kids aren't any better. They act bored with the proceedings, then focus their attention on those electronic devices they can't live without.

Overly permissive parenting, you'll bite your tongue not to say as you issue the holiday ultimatum: "Behave yourselves or we bring out the fruitcake." Maybe the kids' table wasn't such a bad idea after all.

The Twelve Days of Christmas in Grandparentland

Have fun with your grandkids singing these new lyrics to the classic song.

On the first day of Christmas, my grandkids gave to me . . . a million cartoons on DVD

On the second day of Christmas, my grandkids gave to me . . . two dirty socks and a million cartoons on DVD

And so on for days three through twelve . . .

three French fries

four appalling words

five bathtub rings

six laughing lizards

seven Play-Doh pizzas

eight stinky stinkbugs

nine pink piñatas

ten gargling goldfish

eleven giant gumballs

twelve dizzy ducklings

Family Ties

Whether it's Christmas, Hanukkah, Kwanzaa, Chinese New Year, or any of those other big days you reserve for your grandchildren, you'll frequently spend them in the company of your son's or daughter's spouse's relatives.

Keep telling yourself these people are in-laws, not outlaws, no matter how much you think they're stealing precious moments that you might have spent with your grandkids or conspiring to make their family's holiday rituals seem more festive than yours.

Given time, you might even come to like these complete strangers who are now part of your life forever. You'll have plenty of opportunity to get to know each other better as you attend christenings, birthday parties, recitals, school pageants, Fourth of July

bicycle parades, Easter egg hunts, quinceañeras, graduations, and more. Try to keep an open mind because, really, these people couldn't be any weirder than your family.

In fact, this blending of families can be a growing experience for everybody when it brings in-laws of different cultures together. That's when you find the Patels sharing Diwali sweets with the Donahues, or the Nguyens dancing the torah with the Steins. Next weekend the Garcias and the Changs are co-hosting a great big family picnic in the park, complete with posole stew and dumplings.

When both sides of the family are all smiles as they watch  one-year-old Alyssa digging into her smash cake or six-year-old Ryan and his friends enjoying the bounce house and the clown, you have to wonder why countries the world over don't employ grandkids as their diplomats.

These shared cutie pies might be the key to the one gift that everybody wants most for the holidays: Peace on Earth.

Chapter 15
Staying Young and Other Grandparental Endeavors

♫ *May your heart always be joyful*
May your song always be sung
May you stay forever young. ♫

~Bob Dylan

lower children. Deadheads. Yuppies. Grandparents? Like students bewildered by the SAT question that asks which word doesn't belong in the list, we baby boomers keep wondering how *grandparent* crept onto our résumé.

As much as we loved our own grandpas and grandmas, we couldn't help noticing they were sorely out of date. Their clothes seemed old-fashioned, their expressions passé. We found it hard to relate when they talked about dance marathons, Model Ts, and flagpole sitting. Surely the good old days they so fondly recalled had happened an eon or two before we arrived on the scene.

Thanks to our lasting hipness and A-to-Z involvement in nearly everything our grandkids do, we know they could never see us as we saw the parents of our parents. Or so we tell ourselves as we harmonize with The Drifters or Four Seasons on oldies radio en route to an early-bird dinner with friends.

Besides, our grandkids are too smart to let a bit of generational distance come between them and the best all-around playmates/babysitters/taxi service/confidantes/piggy bank/cheering section they'll ever have.

Looking at things chronologically, we know we've entered a new life stage, and some in our ranks already have the Social Security checks to prove it. But there's no doubt we still know where it's at. Just look at all the big-name boomers who remain at the top of their game.

The Boomers-Still-Got-It Hot List
(to name only a few and in no particular order)

Meryl Streep • Denzel Washington • Diane Sawyer* • John Grisham
Bruce Springsteen • Barbie** • Steven Spielberg • Ellen DeGeneres
Whoopi Goldberg • Bruce Willis • Stevie Nicks • Bill Clinton***
Bill Gates • Amy Tan • Dennis Miller • And, of course, YOU!

*Honorary boomer, born only ten days before official baby boom began.
**This chick never seems to age.
***Actually looks better with white hair.

Ponce de Le Who?

Now that we of the original youth culture have morphed into grandparents, the line between young and old doesn't seem so clearly drawn. When we play Hungry Hungry Hippos with young Kylie and Quan or challenge Mia to a *Toy Story* or *Spider-Man* video game, we don't feel all that different than we did when we were their age.

That's because the *me* deep inside each one of us remains a boomer kid at heart no matter how many candles we blew out on our last birthday cake. Even so, we'd gladly climb aboard Mr.

Peabody's WABAC machine and set the dial to, say, thirty-five, which seems a lot younger now than it did when we were there.

As we interact with our grandchildren, we get that

time-machine lift because their youthful enthusiasm has a way of rekindling our own.

We click with these kids on so many levels, from our mutual fondness for Harry Potter, Snickers bars, and *Charlotte's Web* to being in complete accord regarding how irritating their parents can sometimes be.

But no matter how many smartphones we acquire, how often we exercise, or how much we jazz up our vocabulary with words such as *homey, props,* and *wassup,* our grandkids will never mistake us for young. We'll have to keep doing that for ourselves.

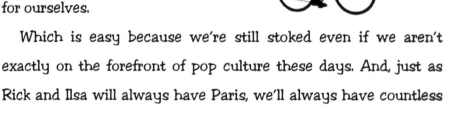

Which is easy because we're still stoked even if we aren't exactly on the forefront of pop culture these days. And, just as Rick and Ilsa will always have Paris, we'll always have countless boomer memories to share.

Remember . . .

Simon and Garfunkel Dy-no-mite Cream Dirty Harry

Alice's Restaurant UNDER MY THUMB Fire and Rain LOVE AMERICAN STYLE

NILSSON

SHAFT M*A*S*H Mrs. Robinson A CHORUS LINE THE FONZ

Richard Pryor

ANNIE HALL Blood, Sweat and Tears The Way We Were na-nu na-nu American Pie

Peter, Paul and Mary Imagine Two wild and crazy guys Me and Bobby McGee taxi driver R2-D2 and C-3PO Nights in White Satin GROK

GARP panty raids Animal House

Bonnie and Clyde OKIE FROM MUSKOGEE PURPLE HAZE UP WITH PEOPLE

Monday Night Football Route 66

Heart of Glass

BUTCH AND SUNDANCE Alfred E. Neuman Willie and Waylon

Farrah Fawcett's swimsuit poster MacArthur Park Mr. Bill HARD-HEADED WOMAN

SATURDAY NIGHT FEVER

Sgt. Pepper's Lonely Hearts Club Band

ROSEANNE ROSEANNADANNA Toodles I ♥ NY SNOOPY California Dreamin'

The Divine Miss M SURFIN' PROUD MARY CHARLIE BROWN Rikki Don't Lose That Number

The Man from U.N.C.L.E. Hello, Muddah Hello, Fadduh CHANGES IN LATITUDES CHANGES IN ATTITUDES

GOODBYE YELLOW BRICK ROAD USA THE PETER PRINCIPLE Goodnight, John-Boy BRIAN'S SONG

Tiny Tim and Miss Vicki Blazing Saddles Blame It on the Bossa Nova

141

Not that we all love every bit of nostalgia memorialized on the preceding page. Naturally, each boomer has a slightly different list because we pride ourselves on being highly individualistic.

That's why some of us picked Door Number One, others Door Number Two. And some chose not to pick at all.

There were boomers who were big on e. e. cummings' poetry, even spelling their names in lowercase letters for a while. Others were totally enthralled with Rod McKuen's verse and made their romantic summer pilgrimages to Stanyan Street.

One boomer quirk that anthropologists are still trying to get to the bottom of is how a small group of us idolized both Black Sabbath *and* Barry Manilow. Sadly, these devotees have never been rewarded with that landmark concept-album collaboration they'd hoped for: *Mandy Does Metal.*

Quiz No. 8: Boy, What a Crooner

Match the singers with their sixties and seventies hit songs.

1. Neil Sedaka	a. Unchain My Heart
2. Glen Campbell	b. Stand by Me
3. Otis Redding	c. Doctor My Eyes
4. Jackson Browne	d. Oh, Pretty Woman
5. Ray Charles	e. Gentle on My Mind
6. Neil Diamond	f. Calendar Girl
7. John Denver	g. Light My Fire
8. Roy Orbison	h. Back Home Again
9. Ben E. King	i. Solitary Man
10. José Feliciano	j. The Dock of the Bay

We Really Did Get Here from There

Watching our grandchildren grow reminds us that it's one quick trip to the other end of the timeline.

Tell your grandson you've been friends with Jim for forty-five or fifty years, and the child will stare at you open-mouthed. He can't begin to comprehend this fact, but it comes as quite a shock to you, too.

Or, if you're surfing TV channels with your granddaughters and happen to mention that there were only three stations when you were a child—all of which signed off every night—they'll say you must be joking.

There's just no getting around it: times have changed, the world has changed, and we've become grandparents. Which means that somehow, somewhere, no matter how much we thought it could never happen to us, we boomers managed (gulp!) to get older. But if we learned anything on the way, it's that every age is a groove when it's ours.

At Home in Grandparentland

As sure as Lassie always found a way to save the day and Perry Mason almost never lost a case, our boomer cool is still securely intact.

However, with vast numbers of younger people coming along behind us, not to mention the effects of gravity, it starts to sink in that we really are getting on in years.

One good thing, for the most part at least, we've stopped worrying about what other people think of us. Whether we peaked early or we were late-bloomer boomers, everything's evened out now. If only that wisdom had come in time to avoid all our teenage angst.

> ### GRANDMA KNOWS
>
> *"The whole circle of life makes sense to me now."*
>
> ~Evelyn *"Grandma" McLean*
> *Fountain Valley, California*

Now, just knowing that we're the one and only Mommers or Poppers to those special little someones is more than enough to make our day. Our week. Our year.

Read *The Little Prince* and *Oh, the Places You'll Go!* to your grandchildren, and ask them to tell you about their hopes and dreams. Then share some of yours because kids should know that grammies and

grampies have hopes and dreams, too. Especially when it comes to their grandchildren.

When you play games together, don't feel you have to let Liam and Avery win all the time to avoid bruising their little egos. Before you know it, they'll be beating you on their own anyway.

Grandparenting Is . . .

➢ A reality show full of comedy, drama, action, and suspense.

➢ A bunny slope compared to the Mount Everest of parenting.

➢ Proof positive that love at first sight really happens.

➢ The job you would never outsource.

➢ Why you'll take even more pictures than Annie Leibovitz.

➢ The opportunity to see your children in a new light.

➢ Your perpetual excuse to go shopping.

➢ The true test of your ability to hold your tongue.

➢ The do-over all parents deserve.

➢ More gratifying than you ever imagined.

If it's true you're only as old as you feel, maybe baby boomers really will stay young forever. We've certainly done a good job of it so far, and having grandchildren is a step in the right direction.

So the next time these kids make you crazy or say something so sweet it brings tears to your eyes, don't be surprised if you realize that Grandparentland is right where you belong.

Answers
to
Quizzes
and
Puzzles

1. Grandparents on TV

1. c.   2. c.   3. a.   4. b.   5. d.   6. b.   7. a.   8. d.   9. c.   10. d.

2. Name That Boomer

1. c.   2. b.   3. c.   4. a.   5. d.   6. b.   7. c.   8. b.   9. c.   10. a.

3. Those TV Words We Couldn't Wait To Hear

1. d.   2. h.   3. g.   4. c.   5. a.   6. e.   7. i.   8. b.   9. j.   10. f.

4. The Grandparentland Permit Exam

Don't worry. Permits aren't really required. But unless you selected "d" for at least three of the five questions, report to Grandparentland Training Camp ASAP.

5. It's All in the Games

1. b.   2. b.   3. d.   4. c.   5. b.   6. c.   7. c.   8. b.   9. d.   10. d.

6. The Plot Thickens

1. h.   2. f.   3. a.   4. j.   5. i.   6. b.   7. c.   8. e.   9. d.   10. g.

7. Sing It, Sister

1. i.   2. e.   3. j.   4. g.   5. b.   6. a.   7. f.   8. c.   9. d.   10. h.

8. Boy, What a Crooner

1. f.   2. e.   3. j.   4. c.   5. a.   6. i.   7. h.   8. d.   9. b.   10. g.

1. Sold!

Master answer: MORRIS THE CAT

2. One, Two, Buckle My Shoe

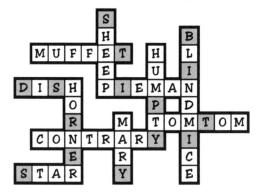

Master answer: ITSY BITSY SPIDER

148

3. Some Things Never Change

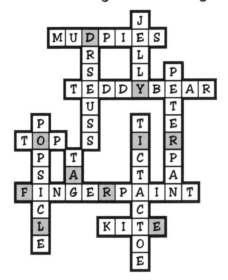

Master answer: RADIO FLYER

4. Baby-Boomer Firsts in History

Master answer: STEVIE WONDER

5. Ooh, What a Dreamboat

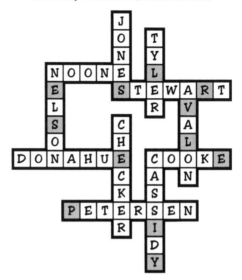

Master answer: ELVIS PRESLEY

6. Where To Go, What To Do

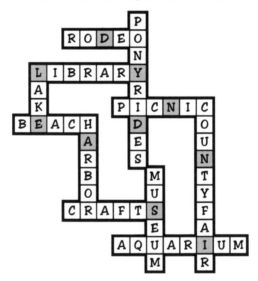

Master answer: DISNEYLAND

7. Oh, Brother, That Guy Can Play

Master answer: MICHAEL JORDAN

Acknowledgments

Many thanks to all the friends and family who encouraged me and provided insights during the course of this lengthy project, particularly Nancy Burley, who planted the seed of an idea by becoming a grandma; MaryAnn Easley, who shared her writing and publishing wisdom; Evelyn Alan for her gentle nudging; Dana Jackson for being both designer and friend; and the Professional Writers Meetup Group with its fearless leader, Michael Varma.

I am deeply indebted to the scores of people who took time to complete my grandparenting survey, including many who are quoted by name in the book and others who offered thoughts and stories anonymously.

In an age when the Internet puts virtually all knowledge at our fingertips, I would be remiss not to mention Google, Wikipedia, and the numerous other websites that served as my always-open reference room and without which this book would not have been possible. I also am grateful to the talented artists whose stock illustrations from Dreamstime.com bring the book's interior to life.

Finally, heartfelt thanks to my husband, David, for his patience and support, even as he had good reason to wonder if "my baby" would ever be delivered.

Permissions

FLY LIKE AN EAGLE
Words and Music by Steve Miller
Copyright © 1976 by Sailor Music
Copyright Renewed
All Rights Reserved Used by Permission
Reprinted by permission of Hal Leonard Corporation

SHOP AROUND
Words and Music by Berry Gordy and William "Smokey" Robinson
© 1960, 1961 (Renewed 1988, 1989) JOBETE MUSIC CO., INC.
All Rights Controlled and Administered by EMI APRIL MUSIC INC.
All Rights Reserved International Copyright Secured Used by Permission
Reprinted by permission of Hal Leonard Corporation

THE NAME GAME
Words and Music by LINCOLN CHASE and SHIRLEY ELLISTON
Copyright © 1964 (Renewed) by EMBASSY MUSIC CORPORATION (BMI) and
  EMI AL GALLICO MUSIC CORP.
All Rights for the U.S.A. Administered Jointly
All Rights for the World outside the U.S.A. Administered by EMI AL GALLICO
  MUSIC CORP. (Publishing) and ALFRED PUBLISHING CO., INC. (Print)
International Copyright Secured. All Rights Reserved.
Used by Permission of EMBASSY MUSIC CORPORATION and ALFRED MUSIC
  PUBLISHING CO., INC.

ANTICIPATION
Words and Music by Carly Simon
Copyright © 1971 Quackenbush Music Ltd.
Copyright Renewed
All Rights Reserved Used by Permission
Reprinted by permission of Hal Leonard Corporation

157

Made in the USA
Lexington, KY
13 June 2013